∾ CalcuDating ∾
Your Single Days Are Numbered

CalcuDating

Your Single Days Are Numbered

Lorraine Adams

Co-written with Jane Hamilton

———

Part of the 'Life Coaching 4' Series

Copyright ©2010 Lorraine Adams
Published in 2010 by SRA Books

SRA Books
Sue Richardson Associates
Minerva Mill Innovation Centre
Station Road
Alcester
Warwickshire B49 5ET
T: 01789 761345
www.suerichardson.co.uk

A CIP record for this book is available from the British Library.

ISBN 978-0-9567553-1-5

Designed, produced and published by Sue Richardson Associates

Printed and bound in Great Britain by TJ International, Padstow, Cornwall

≈ *Acknowledgements* ≈

A huge big thank you goes to my dear friend and co-writer Jane for all her fabulous input into making this book totally reader friendly. Her ideas and direction have been enormously helpful and her positive, hard working attitude is inspiring.

I would also like to thank my gorgeous fifteen-year-old daughter for always bringing me down to earth with a bump by reminding me how embarrassing, annoying, old and wrinkly I am. I'd also like to thank my wonderful partner Brian for being such a great cook and whipping me up fantastic dinners from nothing when I've been so busy working that I've not even had time to visit the supermarket.

My lovely parents definitely deserve a mention for inviting me over to their breathtakingly beautiful house in Spain where I wrote most of this book in the tranquil warmth of the sun with the only interruptions being my mum's lovely regular cups of tea.

I would also like to thank my wonderful girlfriends, amazing women each and every one of them.

∾ *Contents* ∾

Introduction

Introduction

Finding 'The One' is probably the most daunting challenge a woman can face. Whether you're a CEO of an international firm or stacking shelves at the supermarket, your problems are the same. Shall I call him? Did I sleep with him too soon? What does his text really mean? When can we move in together? Single women spend an average of three hours a day analysing every move they make in the game of love; and then there are the sleepless nights fretting about their latest fledgling romance – or the lack of one.

While being on your own isn't the end of the world, most of us would rather be one happy half of a cosy couple. You have already taken a giant step to getting where you want to be just by purchasing this book. I can give you my assurances that in a matter of months your life could be turned around completely, if you are genuinely prepared to take steps, and even leaps, into the unknown, and put everything into becoming a disciple to my Life Coaching for Romance (LCFR) programme. We shall embark on this journey together. I'll guide you right the way through until one day you wake up and know you have arrived. At that stage you may not have found 'The One', but you will feel so self-assured and relaxed and happy with all your new-found knowledge, you will be a 'romance in waiting'.

The author

Let me introduce myself. My name is Lorraine Adams and I'm one of the UK's top romance experts, often dubbed 'The Simon Cowell of Dating'. Why? Because, just like Simon, I don't take any prisoners when it comes to telling it how it is. I'll talk tough with you when it comes to your romantic life and tell you exactly where you are going wrong. You may not like all you hear, and you will experience moments of frustrations when my advice makes you want to explode with anger that life is just not fair, but stick with me and you will find romance – guaranteed.

If you were to hire me privately I'd cost you thousands of pounds, but here in my book I'll share all I know about finding, and keeping, a great man. With hundreds of successful marriages under my belt, and lots of bouncing babies from couples I've set up worldwide, I know following my unique CalcuDating System and by embarking on my LCFR programme you will become another of my romance success stories. Whatever you are going through, whatever you have been through,

I've been there, or had a client who has, and I know exactly how to help.

I chose to write this book because I was tired of, and even shocked by, some of the poor romance advice doled out by magazines and some so-called experts. Single women are often completely wrong footed and that's what I aim to change with my straight-talking, effective advice. What my LCFR programme does that is different is:

- It considers the emotional state of a woman's mind in times of romantic turmoil. While some of the advice currently available may look good on paper, and sound sensible, as I am sure you have experienced at some point in your life, logic disappears in certain complicated romance situations.

- It addresses instinctive male and female behaviour patterns rather than simply accepts the way society tells us we should be thinking, feeling and reacting, even if it goes completely against the grain.

Everything you'll read in my book is objective and based upon years of experience seeing what really works in the world of romance. My style of romance coaching is utterly unique. While some of what I say can be hard to take, my aim is not to crush the life out of you, but to explore what's going wrong and work on enhancing what you have got going for you. When working through my LCFR programme you will analyse why you personally have not been as successful as you would have liked in romance; you will learn how to change your negative patterns of behaviour; and you will discover what else you can incorporate into your personality and your day-to-day life to attract the right types of men for you. I promise I do it with warmth and a positive attitude, and with your best interests at heart.

You may be wondering what's so great about Lorraine Adams. Why do I think I can tell you where you are going wrong when friends, colleagues, and even your family, haven't been able to help you? Let me tell you my story and you'll see.

I didn't actually really start dating properly until the age of 36 when I suddenly found myself single after a 17-year romance. Hopelessly naive, my friends nicknamed me the 'born again virgin', as I'd only ever had one partner after falling head-over-heels in love as a teenager. I approached men as I did as an 18-year-old, with the simplicity of a dizzy teen and a pair of rose-tinted glasses clamped firmly over my eyes. I'd had my fair share of male attention during the years I was loved up, so I sweetly assumed that as a vibrant, slim, sexy 30-something I would be snapped up within weeks and I'd immediately settle down with someone new.

How wrong I was! Men seemed evasive, tricky, and either full of themselves or downright liars. The harder I tried, the less success I had. So I did what so many single women do, I chased harder. Being back on the singles scene after such a long break was brutal, and I literally watched my self-esteem trickle away as my efforts to land a man failed miserably.

Despite living in a fashionable area of London and running my own successful PR firm, I felt having a man would validate me and give me meaning. During my only relationship I'd felt almost defined by the man I was with and the lifestyle I was living. I desperately wanted to be part of a couple again – for my own peace of mind and my two-year-old daughter.

In the late 90s Internet dating was almost unheard of, so I tried placing an advert in a newspaper lonely-hearts column. The result was weeks spent fending off strange stalkers. Next I considered joining a traditional matchmaking agency, hoping they'd hunt me down a husband. However, when I began researching which one would be the best for me, I realised how much these firms were letting singles down. It seemed that most of the conventional dating agencies either had a serious shortage of suitable men or they only catered for the 'desperately seeking'. All I wanted was a decent bloke and it just seemed like there was nothing and nobody out there to help me, no matter how much money I was prepared to throw at them.

I persevered and carried on dating under my own steam. I became a little tougher and more assertive along the way, not allowing myself to feel so deflated when potential little romances faltered at the first hurdle. My confidence began to grow again and my knowledge of what made men tick expanded. However, as I edged towards 40, I was no further towards settling down again. Urgent action was required and there seemed only one logical solution — I'd have to start my own dating club but run it like I wanted a dating agency to be run. I wanted to create something utterly different to anything ever seen before.

Right from the start, I was clear about who my target market would be: I only wanted to attract the interesting, vibrant, go getters into my dating club; the kind of men I'd want to marry and women I'd want to be best friends with. Working in PR I knew all about the 'door policy' where ordinary members of the public were barred from the VIP areas of clubs and bars, so I decided to set up a VIP-only dating agency, with its own door policy. My dating club had to be for the best; for 'gorgeous people' – and so my own dating concept Gorgeous Get-togethers was born.

The agency hit the market in 2000 and the press went wild. Newspapers, magazines, radio and TV stations all ran features on the agency, and my phone rang off the hook with sassy, successful singles wanting to join and have me match them up with equally gorgeous people. Don't get me wrong; it wasn't just about model looks. I wanted to draw a captivating crowd into my network. To me, 'gorgeous' conjures up every aspect of an appealing person, and the most gorgeous aren't always the best looking. The marketing strapline on my Gorgeous Get-togethers website said the service was aimed at those with 'Looks, Presence and Drive', which to me said it all.

With a growing database of thousands looking for love, I very quickly took the plunge into running live dating events. I'd heard about a matchmaking concept, from the New York Jewish community, where men and women who wanted to marry were sent on a series of very short 'mini dates', and so I decided to adapt the idea for the UK. In the same year as setting up the agency, I set up the first European 'speed dating' event with a magazine. Together, the features team and I set up a famous 'IT' girl to meet several of my members and spend just minutes with each before she determined who was worth seeing again for a proper date.

Many of my gorgeous members were 'cash rich but time poor' and wanted to find love fast. At my regular weekly speed dating events my clients met eight prospective new partners. The concept was an instant hit and the media lapped it up. With regular appearances on TV and in magazines and newspapers, my skills were in demand in both the UK and Europe. Within a year my database of über cool singles was large enough to start an online chat and dating site – 'Gorgeous Networks.com'. The members ranged in age from late 20s through to early 40s, and the site is still growing today. Within a few years I'd gone from a terrified newly-single to a successful 40-something with a serious business on my hands and a string of stunning men on my arm. I'd never looked or felt better, and I knew I'd found my calling in life.

Always at the cutting edge of the dating industry, I've pioneered the world's most exciting dating concepts including Hologram Dating, Aphrodisiac Dating, the Wing Woman Service and Wife Auditions. In 2007, I launched Top Dream Dates, a dating site with a difference. More of a social club than a dating site, it's like a lastminute.com concept but for love. Singles can describe their dream date, from hot air ballooning to a weekend at an exclusive spa, and hook up with others who will offer them that experience.

I still get as much of a thrill today as I did ten years ago when I match a couple, and I'm proud to be able to say that I have become the UK's foremost romance expert. My office is crammed with thousands of letters from couples telling me what an amazing difference I have made to their lives.

My dating credentials

It's all very well sorting out the romantic lives of others, but do I practise what I preach? How has my own love life panned out? I'm the first to admit, during the last twelve years since the break-up of my long-term romance with the father of my child, that it's been 'colourful'. In my first four years as a single woman I actually learned so much about myself and about men. I dated a variety of men including a number of sexy, younger men, who, while they looked great and were lots of fun, also taught me some invaluable lessons on how my behaviour and my actions and reactions could win or lose me a boyfriend.

During my 17-year love affair I'd been sweet, accommodating and attentive, but I began to realise during this period of dating that this didn't always bring you what you wanted from a relationship or indeed from your man. The seeds of my LCFR programme were being sown, and how I could be a success when it came to romance all became transparently clear to me.

In 2002, I met a fascinating man, ten years my senior. He was a multi-millionaire who ran, what was at the time, one of the UK's largest dating groups. A journalist had written an article on romance for an up-market magazine, and this successful businessman, who thought himself a hot shot in the field of dating, was furious that out of a six-page article only one page was written about him – the rest of the article was about my radical new ideas. 'Who the hell is this upstart?' he demanded, tearing into the writer. However, after seeing my photo in the magazine, eyes sparkling, he got a message to me to invite me to lunch – on his private yacht that was moored off the coast of Palma Majorca!

How could I refuse an invitation like that? So a few weeks later I was dining on the deck of an amazing yacht, being entertained by this larger-than-life, charismatic, if somewhat overweight gentleman. Never in a million years at that point did I think we'd get together romantically, but his love of life won me over. At first we became business partners; he was eager to hear how he could turn his flagging group of dating sites and agencies around and make them as exciting as mine. Gradually, as our passion for the business grew so did our passion for each other, and we embarked on a sizzling romance together.

He appointed me as a director on the board of his dating group, which had been launched on the AIM stock market months before. I travelled the world first class troubleshooting for his companies and spent the weekends at exotic five-star hotels or languishing on his yacht in the Mediterranean with my young daughter. Within months, my new man and I were engaged and life seemed perfect – or so I thought. Just two years after meeting, my dynamic fiancé was killed in a tragic helicopter accident. I was utterly devastated. How could this wonderful man be taken from me just when I thought my life was turning around again?

Not one to feel sorry for myself, I became single minded and channelled my grief into my work. He had taught me so much about business, and work was all I was interested in for a time; men were completely off the agenda.

It took about a year for me to fall in love again with a man I met in my gym. We exchanged a few glances, which developed over a couple of weeks to light-hearted chatting. He was confident but a little shy, so I left my number with the receptionist at the gym with instructions for her to pass it on to him. He got it, called me and we haven't looked back – I know I've found my soul mate, the love of my life. We've had our ups and downs, but I firmly believe that any relationship with such strong passions will always have highs and lows. It's not for everyone; some people will settle for a more harmonious union, and that's all good too. We all have different energy flows and need to find partners who suit us on our level to ensure long-term happiness.

Through the security of my current relationship, I've spent the last five years taking my business to a new level, fine-tuning my LCFR programme and CalcuDating System. I've also set up a new personal introductions concept, namely Coffee and Company. It's simple but very effective. Every first date I set up for my clients is for coffee only. It's a first impressions date to see if it could be worthwhile taking things further without the toe-curling embarrassment of a blind dinner date with someone you have no empathy with. Why endure hours of uncomfortable conversation when you could save time and heartache by meeting everyone initially just for coffee?

Following this initial introduction, my team and I give clients welcome feedback to help them decipher the intricate language of love. Did he like me? Does he want to see me again? At the end of a coffee date, if you are still in the dark about how it went, we are there to put you in the picture. While we don't relay word for word what clients say about each other, we can give out a general feeler as to whether it's a non-starter or worth holding out for.

All my 'daters' go through a gruelling one-hour 'Personal Evaluation Session' before embarking on any dates, so we can explore the reasons why romance isn't coming their way naturally. Conducting a personal evaluation is the first step in my LCFR programme, so you'll find out more on this as you read through my book.

CalcuDating and the LCFR programme

I decided to write this book to give every unattached girl out there hope. I know what it's like to be knocked back, to be sitting by the phone waiting for the call that never comes, or to want someone who doesn't want you back – I've come through it all triumphant with a wonderful partner and a ring on my finger. I've gone from fling to ring and my aim is to do that for you too.

I chose to team up with my co-writer, journalist Jane Hamilton, who was *The Sun* newspaper's dating correspondent for six years. After a hopeless seven-year relationship failed, Jane took my advice and was engaged to her new partner within six months. She is now married and has a son.

Through her work, Jane has written hundreds of articles on dating trends and tried every type of dating going, including my LCFR programme and my CalcuDating System, so she knows first-hand how it works. Working with me, she has tried and tested each and every step, and together we have refined it so it slots seamlessly into your busy everyday life. We give you this promise: however long you've been single, no matter what age you are or what you do for a living, the LCFR programme can help you, and here's how:

- Starting the programme will help you recognise, understand and eliminate all the unhelpful patterns of behaviour you may have fallen into.

- The CalcuDating System will give you a clear direction to head in and the tools to get there.

- The LCFR programme will bring out the very best in you – mentally, physically and emotionally – and you will begin to identify every area of your life where you may be failing to make an impact with the opposite sex.

- Following the LCFR programme will help you make the most out of every romantic opportunity that comes your way and will ensure you go on dates with the correct attitude so you stand out among your contemporaries.

- You'll become the woman men want to be with and will be wise enough to choose the best partner for yourself instead of settling for second (or third or fourth) best for the sake of being in a relationship.

- You will be better equipped to sustain a relationship.

Although falling in love is never an exact science, the bedrock of the LCFR programme is a unique scoring system, the CalcuDating System. There is a Match Points target you are aiming for and you earn points for every positive action you take towards finding romantic bliss and lose points for falling into bad behavioural patterns that hinder your progress. And when you don't complete the tasks we set for you, you simply don't earn any points. The benefit for you is that it makes my advice measureable; at every step of the way you know exactly where you are on your quest to find Mr Right.

We all think that our love life situation – or the lack of a love life – is completely unique. We empathise and relate to case studies we read, but we all believe that nobody else has to battle with our own particular predicament. All I can tell you is that following my CalcuDating System and the LCFR programme will help any woman in any situation find romantic bliss. If you stick to the plan; if you have a good attitude to changing your bad habits; and if you are open minded and not in denial, you will find romantic happiness.

How the book works

The first part of this book is divided up into four sections:

Part One is the self-evaluation section. You need to put yourself through this process to find out what stage of romance development you are at currently. Many of us think we know, so this section will be very significant and telling.

Part Two is the section where I will reveal to you what I have discovered during my ten-year stint in the romance industry and I share with you the secrets of how to unlock the goddess within. Oh she is there, if you delve deep enough.

Part Three will take you through my unique 'CalcuDating' points system and explain how it all works. Following the CalcuDating System will help you to measure your progress – or deviations!

Part Four starts you on my LCFR programme, showing you exactly what you'll need to do and how the tasks and new disciplines I introduce into your daily routine will make a massive impact on your love life for the better.

The second section of the book is divided into nine chapters that will:

- Help keep you on track and with a positive outlook.

- Keep you from falling at hurdles.

- Teach you all you need to know to get from 'fling to ring'.

But before we start, you need to promise me that you'll really work at finding your future partner. No matter how good I am at what I do, even I can't wave a magic wand and conjure up your Prince Charming. I can tell you how to do it, but the only one who can make it happen is YOU and that will take effort with a capital 'E'.

Your journey starts here – best of luck.

Lorraine

Lorraine Adams

❧ Part One ❧

Tough love – your self-evaluation

Part One Tough love – your self-evaluation

Never before has there been so many single people. Today a staggering 14.2 million Brits are without a partner – but more than half of these are desperately looking for a long-term relationship.

Worryingly, the number of single women in the UK has doubled in the last 30 years – and it is still rising. A frightening 51 per cent of women under 50 have never been married and one in five will never have children. Around one-third of unmarried women are living with a partner, but many co-habiting relationships are short-lived, lasting a couple of years or less. These shocking statistics are set against evidence that now, more than ever before, women want to marry. Nine out of ten young women claim getting a ring on their finger is a major goal in life.

However, when it comes to dating the UK is the least confident country in the Western world. Despite millions of sources of advice from self-help books, to Internet advice sites, magazines and TV shows, half of all single women claim to be held back by a crippling lack of confidence and know-how when it comes to having a successful love life. So where are we all going wrong?

In well over a decade of bringing happy couples together, I've become fascinated by the science of attraction. It never fails to stun me how perfectly compatible couples have a great time on a date, then talk themselves out of taking it further because of peer pressure. Even though they got a nice feeling early into their meeting, they worry their date won't meet the approval of their friends or they think their suitor had one or two tiny things amiss.

I have found that women are far worse than men for this, and get pickier as they get older. I've seen girls reject great guys for silly reasons such as they have unflattering haircuts or because they didn't like their style of shoes; some have rejected men because they don't think their career paths particularly match.

So I ask you to be honest with yourself. If you're hitting 40 without a ring on your finger, is the problem a lack of decent men or could it be you are far too fussy or far too pushy? Are you someone who instantly rejects a man who is earning a good wage and wants to be a dad before you've given yourself a chance to explore the more positive aspects to his personality, just because you don't like his haircut, the places he goes drinking or the car he drives?

If you are the sort of woman who constantly screams 'next', then maybe it's you who has issues? It's my firm belief that our 'Me Me Me' society has a lot to answer for – it certainly has not helped to get couples together to create a 'We' society.

Many women who come to me for help think they deserve a man who looks like George Clooney, cooks like Jamie Oliver, earns at least £100,000 a year, has his own expensive house, a flash car, is faithful and still wants to be home in time for the children's bedtime. If you're thinking like this, the only thing you deserve is a reality check. Spend a few minutes with me thinking about the happiest couples you know. Do they both look like A-listers or earn six-figure salaries? Would you have ever put them together yourself? Possibly not.

The cosiest couples are the ones who compromise, who trade the non-perfect parts of their relationships for the bits that they love about each other. He may have a pot belly or be slightly balding, but if he is a good man and loyal what's not to love? He may be a bit of a flirt, but if he treats you like a queen why look elsewhere? We've all been so brainwashed into believing the only thing we should accept is an airbrushed, Hollywood-style romance, that we've forgotten the real art of attraction.

Some of the best unions I've been responsible for have come through me coaxing two singles to meet – even though neither of them fitted the other's original 'wish list'. If I get a strong sense of synergy between two people, I disregard the 'must haves' and suggest they meet anyway.

I've seen dozens of couples fall deeply in love and tie the knot this way, despite rejecting each other initially based on the strength of a photo or a list of likes and dislikes. Who we fancy and why is down to nature – we can't train ourselves to switch off to one man and on to another, but we can teach ourselves to make the most of every opportunity.

First, however, before you even begin to think about starting your hunt for the perfect romance, I need to take you through two initial stages: my Romance Reality Check and your Personal Self-Evaluation.

Romance reality check

Here's where it starts to get hard. Are you up for the challenge? Do you know how much you want this and if you're tough enough to cope? You've read the statistics at the start of this section, and the chances are that you could be competing for men with anything up to **half** of the other women in your age group. Put simply, singles are waging a war out there, and only the fittest will survive to snatch the prize of marriage. My job is to turn you from an ordinary and average relationship hunter into a member of the SAS group – Sexy, Assured, Sophisticated.

Take a look through my Romance Reality Check below. Think long and hard about each of my four questions, as they will pop up in some shape or form throughout this book. The quicker you are willing to listen and accept what I have to say, the sooner we can get to work.

1) Single is a state of mind. You may believe you hate being single, and can't wait to get coupled up, but how often have you sabotaged what could be a loving relationship before you've even given it the chance to get started?

In my work I meet far too many women who are actually very comfortable being single. They moan about men all the time and blame their own failures in love on the opposite sex, which stops them looking inwards at themselves and what may be wrong. Other women have such busy lives and high-powered jobs that, although they may think they want a partner, they don't devote the time to finding or keeping him. Often I set up a coffee date between two people and suggest a meeting time a week or so ahead, only to find the woman has rescheduled for a month's time – and this is just a coffee date!

If you really want to meet a man, you have to open up your mind and your diary to romance. I won't tolerate women who tell me there are no good men out there or that they're all married, gay, or cheats. What rubbish! If this were the case then none of us would get married when over a quarter of a million of us say 'I Do' each year.

Before you begin to work with me, be honest with yourself. Is being loved-up really what you want? Are you prepared to put the work in? I can only help you if you are prepared to soul search and really make an effort to follow my LCFR programme.

2) Be realistic. So you want to hook Brad Pitt? Fair enough, who doesn't? However, if you don't look like and have the personality, drive and captivating aura of an Angelina Jolie or Jennifer Anniston, then honey, I'm sorry, you don't stand a chance.

You wouldn't believe the number of frumpy, overweight 40-somethings who come to me on a husband hunt, then get upset when the sexiest men on my books aren't interested in them. I read emails time and time again that tell me 'I'm 48 but really I don't look my age' only to discover when I meet them in person that they certainly don't look 48 – they look nearer 58! Elle McPherson doesn't look her age, so trying to delude yourself that you are in her league doesn't wash with me – and it certainly doesn't wash with the eligible guys out there.

It may be brutal, but let's share some tough love here. Unless you are prepared to really work at what you have to offer, you may need to lower your sights. It doesn't mean you won't find a wonderful man, but he may not have absolutely everything you've pictured in your mind and convinced yourself that you want. Many a frog has been kissed only to discover he becomes a prince who will bring you just as much happiness as you're dreamed-up, picture-perfect Mr Right. You need to be with me on this; try to give a man a chance.

To labour this point across to you think about the 80/20 rule: research proves that a huge 80 per cent of couples marry someone they didn't find attractive in the first instance. That's right, no instant fireworks, no light bulb moment and certainly no love at first sight. Just one in five happy couples who have been together for more than five years liked the look of each other when they first met. So if you're the kind of person who dismisses a date on the strength of his photo, believe it or not, you are missing out on four out of five potential partners.

It doesn't take Einstein to work out that if you are being harshly judgemental about small things, this is bad news. My advice is to take the blinkers off. Look beyond the first glance and you will find there are a **lot** of gorgeous guys lurking out there.

3) You get what you give. Now for the good news. Whatever your starting point is in so far as looks, sex appeal, charisma and other assets, you can up your game and dramatically improve your chances of finding someone a little nearer to your idea of perfection.

If you're overweight, get down to the gym and drop the extra pounds and tone up. Not only will you feel better and ooze more confidence and sex appeal, men will notice you more. It may sound obvious, but it will certainly work better for you than lounging on the couch watching *East Enders* with a carton of ice cream. Try being as proactive with your love life as you have been perhaps with your career or other things you have excelled at.

If you work long hours and feel you lack conversation outside of the office, join a weekend club or start a new pursuit to expand your horizons. Smarten up physically and mentally and you'll trade up in no time.

Think of it as a CV for Love. If you start improving what you have to offer, you'll land a better deal. I've never met anyone that can't be upgraded – and that includes me. I worked long and hard to make the very best of myself, and in doing so it has allowed me to enjoy more choice of men.

I know from a decade in this business that Cupid certainly isn't hanging around waiting to fire arrows at you and a handsome stranger. He's more likely to be working his magic on the man you see on the train each day but ignore because he's half an inch too short. Are you ready to remove those blinkers and open your eyes and see what's out there for you?

4) Listen to your heart. We all like to listen to our best friends and families for advice, but I've seen a lot of women talked out of relationships this way. Be honest with yourself – is your best mate putting your date down because she's worried you'll get hitched while she's left on the shelf? Maybe your mum wants you to marry a lawyer and doesn't think your new squeeze's job is up to the grade. If he's a good catch in every other way, then really, who cares what his job title is? You're the one in the relationship with him, not them. You decide.

Now for a word of warning before we really get started: don't run before you can walk. Remember to play the long game in the quest for love. I've lost count of the number of times I've seen my clients listen to my advice and then revert back to their old bad behaviours before they have barely got started. I know you're in a rush to find someone special, and I know you feel you have no time to lose, but patience is the biggest virtue you can have right now.

We need to work together to fix what's gone wrong on your quest for love so far – and flag up what is going right too – this will take a little time. Trust me to be your guide and I'll get you where you want to be, step by step.

The self-evaluation test

The next stage is to take my Self-Evaluation Test. Between us we need to establish where you stand in the 'appeal stakes'. Unfortunately, I see countless women – and men – whose expectations far out-weigh what they have to offer. I always encourage women to reach for the stars when searching for a soul mate, but as I keep saying, 'it's no good trying to attract the most sought-after men when we are unrealistic about what we have to offer in return'.

Yes you may be a nice person, but are you dynamic? Being a nice person will get you a nice, average bloke. By being dynamic and a step ahead of other women, you will have the crème de la crème competing for your heart, as well as countless other eligible blokes.

Take a look at the chart below and ask three people to fill it in. (You can either photocopy from this book or login to www.calcudating.com) Make sure one person is a very honest friend, one is male, and one is someone who doesn't know you quite so well – perhaps a work colleague in another department or a friend of a friend. Don't cheat. The only person you'll be conning is yourself. If you opt for three people who love you warts and all, they may find it too difficult to be truly honest with you.

Your self-evaluation is vital to understand what you need to do to improve your romance rating from the perspective of (a) body, (b) mind and (c) spirit and to make the most of every opportunity. I never take on a client without first going through this stringent evaluation process. Once we know your weaknesses and your strengths, we can put the LCFR programme in progress and take huge steps in the right direction.

Self-Evaluation Report

On a scale of 1 to 5, where 1 is not very good and 5 means among the best you've seen, what mark would you give in the following three areas.
A maximum of 25 points can be given for each category, and each point is worth 4%. For example, 20 points means a score of 80%:

Physical	Points awarded
1. Physique and looks: is she head turning?	
2. Fashion, style, hair, make-up: is it well above average?	
3. Sex appeal, charisma, femininity: is she effortlessly attractive?	
4. Body language: do you notice her when she walks in the room?	
5. Is she energetic and vibrant?	

Physical_____ points_____%

Mental attitude	Points awarded
1. Articulation, humour, spontaneity: is she engaging?	
2. Does she appear to practise positive thinking?	
3. Beliefs and attitude: if over bearing and self-opinionated mark low, if more self-deprecating mark higher.	
4. Does she pose herself as a challenge to men and allow them to do all the running? Mark high for yes.	
5. Interests, hobbies, pursuits: does she appear to have lots going on in her life?	

Mental attitude_____ points_____%

Spiritual and emotional wellbeing	Points awarded
1. Does she have plenty of self-esteem and confidence?	
2. Has she an enthusiasm, passion and drive for life in general?	
3. Is her work–life balance equal in your view?	
4. Is she caring and warm to almost everyone?	
5. Is she accepting and good at adapting? Think about her attitude to change and her listening skills when it comes to change.	

Spiritual and emotional wellbeing_____ points_____%

Evaluation calculations

Once you have the three evaluations back, tally the scores from each category using the total from each evaluator. To get the average, divide the totals of each category by three. If your scores vary enormously from person to person, then consider asking three more people to get a more accurate evaluation. Some people may be too generous; at the same time others may be too hard on you. As mentioned before, it is important that you are careful whom you choose to do the evaluations.

A. Physical   Total_____   Average_____

B. Mental attitude   Total_____   Average_____

C. Spiritual and emotional wellbeing Total_____   Average_____

I know this challenge is exceptionally tough, and may yield answers you don't want to know, but it is important to get you started with a truer picture of where you are. If you really can't face asking your friends and colleagues to evaluate you, see Appendix two for details on how to have a personal evaluation with either me or one of my team of client liaison managers.

Your scores

If your total average combined score is 66+ (out of a possible 75 points)
As long as this was a really honest evaluation, you really have it all. The LCFR programme should prove to be easy for you to follow with almost instant results. It's probably just a case of fine-tuning and you getting a bit of direction. It may be just bad luck or rotten circumstances stopping you finding Mr Right, or maybe you are lacking self-belief and don't realise what you've got. In the past, clients of mine who scored 66 or more are rarely still single after a few months of enlisting my help. Follow my LCFR programme and expect a ring on your finger within the year.

If your total average combined score is 54–63 (out of a possible 75 Points)
You have some way to go, but at least your friends were honest. Analyse which category you lost most points on, and we can work harder to improve them. If it's the physical side, it may take a little longer to lose a few pounds and change

your appearance, but mental attitude and spiritual and emotional wellbeing won't take long to conquer. Soon you can be at the top of your game.

If your total average combined score is 53 or less (out of a possible 75 points)
First off, thank you for being so honest. The outcome may have hurt your feelings, but when you're down with the dumped the only way is up.
You really need to stick to the LCFR programme rigidly to make the big life changes you desire. Invest a few months working on yourself now, and no more years will slip by with you feeling lonely and unloved.
My biggest success stories are clients who have come from rock bottom.
Sure, you may feel like the ugly duckling, but we all know there's a gilded swan inside waiting to glide out.

Let's get going!

~ Part Two ~

Unlocking the goddess within

Part Two Unlocking the goddess within

It's a scene we've all observed. A handsome man is walking along the street with his arm protectively curled around a rather plain woman – but he's gazing at her with adoring eyes like she's the most stunning creature on earth. 'What has she got that I haven't?' we wonder. But I can tell you now, that girl is a goddess. She's unlocked the age-old secrets of how to lure in and create the loveliest of partners.

Once upon a time, these feminine wiles were passed on from mother to daughter. Women were taught to maintain their feminine mystique and seduce any man they wanted – but sadly these exquisite secrets have almost all been lost. In our Jeremy Kyle confessional society, women are encouraged to want it all, tell it all and show it all off! Is it attractive to men? No.

So you want to know the secret of how to attract the best men, even though it actually isn't always evident who the best men are initially? How is it that some women, even those you think don't have as much to offer as you, seem to have the guys falling at their feet, while you never get a look in? Why do some women effortlessly hang on to their men, while everyone you feel yourself falling for walks away before you even get started?

What I'm about to reveal to you is as old as time itself, but somehow many of us have forgotten what actually should be instinctive. Only a true goddess will have learned the secrets of what it takes to bag a fabulous romance and partner. I've tried and tested these pearls of wisdom over the last ten years, and I **know** they work. One or two things I'm about to show you may seem strange, or even go against what you currently believe, but if you follow my advice to the letter you will get to a place where you start to have the pick of any men you want; suddenly you'll find a wealth of men where before the dating landscape seemed to be barren. You won't have to 'settle' for someone or become what you think he wants. You won't be fretting about what you say, do, think or wear, as everything will begin to go with the flow and fit into place. Before you know it, you will find yourself in a great relationship.

Please trust me when I say it will be as easy as that, but you have to become a disciple to the LCFR programme. Disregard some of the advice, or cheat on some of the tasks, and you will only be swindling yourself out of a wonderful romance.

There are just **four** key attributes every woman should possess if she wants to be a hit with men – all men. Forget the superficial, trashy teen magazine tips about flicking your hair and wetting you lips that you've spent your whole life reading. What I have to tell you goes much deeper, yet you will find it much simpler to understand. Every woman has a latent ravishing goddess within, and my Four Golden Keys will unlock her.

First Golden Key: rediscovering your femininity

Probably the most important of all traits a woman should posses in abundance is sex appeal, yet men and women have a very different definition of what sexy means. Many women believe sex appeal is something skin deep. They mistakenly assume that all men ultimately want are glossy lips, short skirts with endless legs, bouncing blonde hair, a heaving cleavage or a 'peachy' bum. The truth is most men find many of these things *sexual*, but they don't necessarily find them *sexy*. Sure, gorgeous long-legged, mini-skirted women will make men stare and big bulging boobs may make him feel turned on, but they aren't the secret of sex appeal – and they certainly aren't at the top of the list when men are looking for a future wife.

So what is it that men really want? The secret to having heaps of sex appeal is very simple – to be *feminine*. But before you rush out to start shopping for a flowing, floral dress, femininity is more of a mindset than how you look. Although being well groomed is certainly attractive to men, women who have a more dishevelled look can still have men entranced by their every move. Let's look at some celebs here:

Victoria Beckham is one of the world's most photographed women and is always turned out immaculately. She has spent millions on matching outfits and looks like she's stepped straight from a fashion catwalk. Do men find her feminine?

Dame Helen Mirren is well into her 60s and has a lined and lived-in face. Do guys find her irresistible? She embraces life, looks like she'd be infectious fun, but always acts like a lady. She's a pure goddess and knows every inch of how to be feminine.

Consider, too, how men the world over drool over French women. Our Gallic sisters are renowned for taking pride and care in their appearance. They prepare, and this is something men find very feminine in a woman. Take the extra trouble to get ready for a date French-style, with matching lingerie and fragrant body cream, even if you are only meeting for a coffee and he doesn't get to see the saucy lingerie. What he will pick up on is an aura of 'all woman' surrounding you simply by the way the preparation has made you feel and present yourself. He will remember your actions and they will hold a place in his heart. Only the other day I popped out in my tracksuit with no make-up, apart from a little lip gloss, to get a newspaper. I was freshly showered, my hair was clean and I was wearing a beautiful rose scented perfume. The man behind me in the queue smiled and commented how beautiful my perfume was. Now I can tell you, I'm an average looking 49 year old. Making an effort is one of the secrets of real sex appeal. Most women are capable of turning on a man, but it takes a special one to get him thinking about her long term.

However, even if you are the sort of woman who is always well turned out, you may still not be feminine enough. It's an acquired attitude; something you may need to work at rather than be able to adopt overnight. Even reading through this section will begin to make you more feminine, as you digest what you read and become aware of what men are ultimately seeking in a woman.

It's a fact that a lack of femininity is the number one cause of men rejecting women after a first date. All too often, the worst offenders at not being able to harness their femininity are hard working successful and powerful career women – and sadly there's no secret as to why. Today women are encouraged to compete viciously with men at work. We have to be rougher, tougher, work longer hours and negotiate harder to get on in what is still essentially a man's world. Rarely do we try to get ahead using our natural womanly charms, for fear of offending colleagues or being seen as feeble. By acting like men when we are really women, we are weakening our natural female magnetism. Instead of seeing femininity as an invaluable tool, we have become accustomed to viewing it as something that could thwart our climb to career success.

Having a competitive nature may be something that works for us career wise, but when it carries on into our private lives it can sometimes be unnecessary and unattractive. Look at it from a man's point of view. A ball-breaker may be OK in the boardroom, but would he want to share a bedroom with her? No. A man is ultimately seeking a wonderful, delicious, delightful woman to love. He doesn't want to share his life with his CEO.

I'm not saying women need to stop being competitive or turn into dull doormats, but we do need to curb our urge to want to control everything. Too many women feel the need to emasculate their man by trying to take over every aspect of his life, from what he wears to managing his career. Others attempt to dominate the pace of the relationship, forcing it into fast forward.

If you're a long-time single girl you'd do well to remember that while most men will enjoy the banter with a 'smart Alec' he doesn't want her for a girlfriend. Being a know-it-all will have a man dump you weeks or even months into your relationship. You may have everything else going for you, but if your feminine traits are not glaringly obvious gradually you will lose your appeal.

We may feel we are the smarter half of the couple and be rightfully proud of our accomplishments, especially if they tower above what the man in our life has managed to achieve, but the feminine woman holds a more sensual and self-deprecating stance. She will never boast about her achievements if it comes across as outshining her man. If you are, or can be, comfortable with this, you will have men falling at your feet.

What you really need to learn to do is 'man-ipulate'. Many view this as a dirty word, but look at the dictionary definition of 'manipulate' and it relays a very positive, powerful word: 'to handle or manage or use skilfully, to arrange or influence cleverly'. That's exactly what I'm asking you to do – to use all your feminine wiles to charm your man. To me, manipulation is a very positive skill. Remember the saying that behind every successful man is a woman driving him? Well it's the manipulative woman who makes her man feel he's the smart one running the show while quietly getting everything she ever wanted – and it's the manipulative woman who keeps her man adoring her. I'm not suggesting that you become submissive or allow your man to take the credit for all your hard work and ideas, but just to allow a man to be a man. He will worship you for it. Sit back and let your achievements be discovered instead of forcing them on people to prove you are a success; it is all about learning to be gracious.

Let's swing it around. When we list the qualities we want in a partner, most of us desire a masculine man. We want him to be rich and powerful, or confident with strength of character. Maybe we want him in a position of authority or big and strong physically? A man with any combination of these attributes will have no trouble attracting women, even if he isn't that good looking. Maybe masculinity isn't something we can define or put our finger on, but we can all spot a masculine man when we see one! And while most of us don't **need** a man to look after us, we all secretly desire a bit of looking after every now and then.

By the same token, a guy does not necessarily **need** a strong woman behind him, but he certainly feels better and more content when he has one. Likewise, while many men struggle to define what constitutes a feminine woman, they will always be attracted to one when he comes across her. In his eyes, before you even speak, he has found a precious prize, and to him you're already head and shoulders above most of the other women in the room. Feminity is one of the most powerful tools a woman can possess. Don't be fooled into thinking that it is about being weak, twee or girly; it is about being **all woman**. Read the chapter on rediscovering your femininity for more tips about rediscovering your womanly charms.

CASE STUDY

Laura is a 37-year-old PA. Growing up with three older brothers, she was always a tomboy. She wore her wild hair cropped short, refused to wear dresses and drank pints on nights out, downing them to 'impress the lads'. While never short of male mates, any man she got close to viewed her as a much-loved friend but never a potential girlfriend.

Laura's so-called pals did nothing to change her and assured her she looked great. Why? They were happy for her to stay the same way, as she brought with her an endless supply of her brothers' eligible friends and was no competition herself.

When Laura came to me I had to shock her into seeing herself as others saw her. There were tears and tantrums, but we worked to rediscover her feminine side. She grew her hair, swapped jeans for slinky dresses and toned down her loud banter and wild side. She stopped trying to manage and boss everyone and adopted a more relaxed, easy-going nature.

In short, she blossomed as a gorgeous woman. Within three months, she was out on dates four nights a week. One year later, Laura was engaged to be married.

Second Golden Key: pose yourself as a challenge to men

Since the dawn of time men have been hunters and this will never change. Men are programmed to go for the chase; to track down the object of their desire. Whether it's his career, saving for a new car or lusting after a new woman, all men need a constant challenge in their lives. It's an innate characteristic of a man to feel that anything worth having must prove difficult to obtain. This includes your love. If a guy feels he hasn't had to 'try hard' to win over **and keep** your affection, then his interest in you wanes. Posing yourself as a challenge should be a lifelong crusade if you want to keep your partner's attention as fresh as when you first met.

Please don't confuse posing yourself as a challenge with challenging your man all the time; be mindful of the fact that your man must always feel he is punching slightly above his weight in your relationship. He has to feel that he is genuinely lucky to have you, and even more so the longer you grow into your relationship and he discovers more of your personality and warmth.

Think hard; what is the first thing most women do when we meet someone who melts our heart? We become all-consumed and too accommodating; we shower him with attention and affection; and we try to rescue him. In an instant, we've gone from dream girl to doormat and have stopped posing ourselves as a challenge.

Many of us can keep him dangling for a few days, even a few weeks, but then we drop down our guard and become a passive pushover, because we believe it's what he wants. And what happens? Suddenly this man, who was so smitten, starts to drift away. His attention to us wanes, and we become even more pushy and less of a challenge.

For many women, it's happened more than once. Yet we fail to recognise the warning signs and fall into the same pattern time and time again. Rather than blame ourselves, we turn it back on the man. How many excuses have you used? I bet you've claimed a former boyfriend as 'commitment phobic', only to see him wed the woman he dated after you. You'll blame it on him not getting over his ex, or that he isn't in the right place emotionally, and then see him happily settle down with someone else? Or do you wail he isn't mature enough, despite the fact he's 35?

You probably don't have any trouble keeping the interest of the guys you don't fancy. They battle to try to win you over, but the more you ignore them the more they come for you. But for some strange reason, you think the guys who appeal to you are going to act differently? Wake up to the reality; it's not him – it's you! You need to back off to give him space to chase.

Even in a long-term relationship you must keep the balance right. Your man needs to feel that he is never quite sure how you are going to react; you need to keep him guessing in small ways every day. A man who doesn't feel there is anything to try hard for in his relationship will seek the challenge elsewhere – sometimes in the arms of other, more interesting women. Even the most loyal and trustworthy men will turn their attentions away from their adoring partner, throwing themselves into work and losing interest in their woman. Or they will become obsessed with outside interests. That's why there are so many frustrated golf widows waiting for their husband to come home!

It is understandable that you want to make a good impression when you are first getting to know a man to show him you're a potential long-term mate, but what you most likely fail to grasp is that he can easily spot the warm aspects of our personality anyway and you don't have to labour every little point at his feet. He will pick up on your kind-heartedness, your considerate nature and your compassion – or whatever it is we are so desperately trying to convince him of – by the way you behave with your friends, colleagues and family.

I find most men I come across and have interviewed say they want a lovely, warm, friendly, easygoing woman; of course they don't tell me they want to be with anyone who is 'difficult'. However, I've matched thousands of men over the years and have seen first-hand that a little bit of 'difficult' has inspired that extra little bit of desire they have for their woman. While I don't want to encourage you to be high maintenance, I do want you to be spirited. Remember, you are the jewel in the crown; his precious prize. Keep him chasing and lusting after you, and you'll keep him keen and interested forever.

Feisty lawyer, Siobhan, 34 year old, had every man she met falling at her feet. A stunning size 8 figure, razor sharp mind and chic dress sense ensured she had the whole package. But she couldn't keep a man for more than a month. Why? When she came to me, it soon became clear that although she was in control of her head, she had no control over her heart.

As soon as any man showed a flicker of interest, Siobhan was so desperate to take it further that she'd mould herself to be what she thought he wanted. She'd take up his hobbies, change her make-up and clothes and even 'accidentally' bump into him when he was out with his mates — even if it meant driving miles to his local. She'd over-analyse every text and phone him angrily if he didn't return her calls within a few minutes. In short, she made herself so easily available that it rapidly became a turn-off.

What man wants a woman who throws herself at him? Guys think if you do it to them, you've done it to every other man in town too. I had to train her to hold back and be less available. It was very hard and went against everything in her nature, but she began to turn it around and make men run after her. She'd claim to be busy so guys couldn't book her in for dates, and tease men with the thought she had a better offer elsewhere.

Two years on, I watched from the back of the church as she walked down the aisle with a husband who thought he'd made the catch of his life. My job was done!

Third Golden Key: self-belief

Do you think women are the weaker sex? Of course not, and neither does any man. Look at the power we hold over men when they're in love with us, or how most men take more notice of their mums than their fathers. Don't delude yourself that men look upon a feminine woman as a weak woman. Every man loves a strong female but strong in a subtle way; not a woman who is brash and bold. The key to being strong is to have bundles of self-belief. A woman with this essential power, who will not fold at the first sign of a drama, is a woman who has a sense of self-worth. If a woman shows that she respects herself, men automatically respect her and believe she's worth fighting for. A woman with low self-esteem spells 'needy' to a guy, and men can smell this neediness a mile off. No man wants to take on a desperate, insecure, vulnerable other half.

You will find the only men who actively seek out the company of women with low self-esteem are the controlling ones, usually because they have a low sense of self-worth themselves. These are the toxic guys who appear to be Mr Marvellous early on in the relationship, as they attempt to prise open your more vulnerable side. This type of man can appear so sympathetic that we can be blinded to his true intentions and find him flattering and endearing. But bearing your soul and divulging you life's woes to a man you barely know will come back to haunt you in the form of a controlling bully, so steer well clear.

Every woman knows her self-esteem levels vary from day to day. One moment she can feel wonderful, the next she'll be down in the dumps or having a 'fat day', depending on what's going on in her world. But don't confuse confidence with self-esteem, as many a strong confident woman has very low self-worth, especially when it comes to men. I have watched a woman deliver a faultless two-hour seminar to over a hundred men, then fall to pieces in the break because she received a hurtful text message from her boyfriend.

My job is to work with you to get you to the point where you don't question yourself and soul search every time a date or budding relationship doesn't go according to plan. There are disciplines for you to follow in this book to bolster your self-esteem if it is lacking a little. Time and time again I see a woman go on an enjoyable first date, and come back believing she's met someone she has a real synergy with. Both parties agree to see each other again and all seems well. But all too soon – and sometimes within an hour of getting home – she starts fretting about when her date is going to call her again. The longer she goes without hearing from him, the more frantic she gets. She'll replay every minute of the date in her mind, wondering what he really meant or whether she should have given a smarter answer. Did she impress him enough for him to want to see her again? Eventually she'll crack and think of an excuse to call or text. And if he doesn't reply immediately, she'll call and text again, even adding a hint of resentment in the text if he hasn't responded.

If this all sounds familiar, and you have found yourself many a time boring your friends silly after your dates, you may be suffering from low self-esteem.

From the man's point of view, if you make contact first it takes the romantic wind out of his sails. He'll feel marginally disappointed in you. He feels conned out of his role of the hunter and less of a man. Without even realising it, you have emasculated him. One essential dating tactic you must understand is that men take time to respond – and it's not because they don't like you; quite the opposite in fact. If a man's keen, he can take days to plan his strategy for wooing you, and even longer to get back in touch.

Often he will withdraw slightly and deliberately not call or text for a few days in the hope that he doesn't come across as too keen and risk losing your interest. At this stage, he secretly hopes that he has stumbled across a feisty, stimulating girl, who poses herself as a challenge so he can forge ahead with winning your affections. But, if you're calling and texting every few hours you've blown it big time. You've made it way too easy and abundantly clear that he doesn't have to even *try* to win you over as you are there ready for him. Believe me, this is the *only* reason men who seemed keen at first simply give up their pursuit.

Men go about life very differently to us women and have no problem compartmentalising each different area of their lives. While we become all consumed after a great date, talking endlessly about it to friends, family and colleagues, a man can go on a date with a girl, then put his feelings on hold while he works out his romantic plan. Men love to draw out the pursuit for as long as they can and savour the thrill of the chase. I've seen guys go up to three weeks between a first date and calling a girl for a second meet up. Why? Well, while you're weeping by the phone wailing to friends how he hasn't called, the guy is in the gym honing his body to try to impress you next time you meet. Or have you ever thought he may be finishing up liaisons with other ladies, leaving him free to concentrate on you? It could be that he may just want to finish a project at work so there's nothing more on his mind but an evening in your company.

If a man finds you attractive and thinks you are out of his league, he'll want to be at his peak the next time you meet – so he'll bide his time until he feels he is at his best. What he won't do is call you within an hour of dropping you home and organise to meet you in two weeks when he is probably going to be feeling in better shape. Even if he feels he can see you again soon, he will rarely want to arrange to meet you for the next five nights, unless it's an urgent sex-only interest, and we all know about those guys.

A woman with self-belief will come away from a date confident that the guy will call eventually – however long that takes. She'll busy herself and put him to the back of her mind until he does, and if he doesn't, she will convince herself he wasn't right for her in the first place, or that it wasn't their time. She certainly won't contact him, fret or moan to friends, and she definitely won't lower herself into an 'accidental' meeting at places she knows he hangs out.

The big problem with many women, and especially British girls, is that they often regard a good date as the beginning of a relationship. Instead of enjoying the date for what it is and being content to perhaps see each other again at some point, some girls are planning the colour of the bridesmaids' dresses half an hour after meeting a new man!

Too many women want to rush things, especially those whose biological clock is ticking loudly. The irony is, by slowing down the pace and stepping back, you'll land a husband far faster than trying date by date to force them into more quick fire dates before they are ready. These women lose out on potential romances time and time again.

Learn to alter your approach and believe in yourself and what you have to offer. If you don't feel you have much to offer, then do something about it; spend your energy on this for a while and put men on the back burner until you do consider yourself a genuine catch. Soon enough your dream man will turn into reality.

Actress Leona, 36, was never short of male admirers. With tumbling dark curls and honeyed skin, she captivated men whether simply shopping in the supermarket or shaking her stuff on the dance floor. However, after every date she'd text to say what a great night she had and how she couldn't wait to see them again. Sometimes she'd even suggest a meeting place, time and venue for later that week.

When she came to me, I cringed at the messages she'd fired off to guys. She thought she was simply being polite and carrying on the evening's conversation, but the men smelled desperation and rarely bothered to get back in touch.

For Leona, I devised an extreme plan with the help of her flat mate Caroline. After every date, Leona would go to Caroline's room and hand over her mobile phone. Caroline would then keep it safe for a couple of days to stop Leona being tempted to send a text or call. The men didn't know, they just thought Leona was playing it cool.

Within six weeks Leona began to see the benefits, so I trusted her to take back her phone. Now three years on she's married, with a young son, and living in America with a man she made chase her for two weeks before their second date.

Fourth Golden Key: be captivating

So, you have strong self-belief, you're feminine in every way and a challenge to every man that crosses your path, but if you want to win over the crème de la crème of the male population you have to be captivating too.

Being captivating is a hard quality to define. It's having that certain *je ne sais quoi* that others warm to and makes people want to spend time in your company. I believe it's about being vibrant and having a passion and enthusiasm for everything you do. It's a sad fact that many single women end up throwing themselves into their work in an attempt to fill the void in their lives.

I see dozens of women each month who tell me 'I have a wonderful life; a man would just be the icing on top of the cake'. When I delve deeper, most of their conversation revolves around their jobs. Having a great career can be part of being captivating, but it's certainly not the be all and end all. Many women devote so many hours of their lives to work, they forget all about taking some 'me time' to do something solely and selfishly for themselves. Indeed, lots of women feel it's a waste of time to introduce themselves to new interests and pursuits, but what they fail to realise is how indulging in a new interest, or learning about something different, brings a wave of vibrancy into their lives.

A woman who is well travelled and well read, a woman who is always going places and doing things, a woman who takes care of her health by exercising regularly and takes pride in her appearance, is a woman who usually has an adoring band of men following her.

When you have plenty going on in your life outside of work, you become a different type of person, without even realising it. You're transformed into a person who has an engaging opinion on a huge repertoire of subjects, you have something intelligent to add to any conversation, and you'll find you regularly strike up your own discussions while you hold court. People are interested in what you have to say because you deliver everything with more passion. Everyone will want to catch your eye and engage your interest. Suddenly, you've gone from all work and no play to the life and soul of the party.

It just takes a little effort to become more interesting, and it pays dividends. A man will pick up on a vibrant woman without even being directly in her company, because she has a natural aura of energy surrounding her. Her presence and enthusiasm is infectious, and he'll be drawn to her instantly. A vibrant woman is one who will light up a room; she's the girl every man wants to talk to and meet.

Now just ponder on this for a moment: imagine your power if you combine your new-found vibrancy with a strong self-belief, heaps of femininity and an awareness that you can pose yourself as a challenge to any man you meet. It will feel fantastic to know you're all woman, with men everywhere wanting to get to know you. At this stage you can simply bide your time, waiting for the perfect romance to fall into your path.

Corporate banker, Eleanor, 29, worked 14-hour days and often at weekends too. Although she was rewarded with an amazing apartment, a six-figure salary and a shiny new sports car, she was exhausted. Her job left her washed out with very little time for looking after herself.

When I began working with Eleanor, I encouraged her to take a little 'me time' each day. What began with a 20-minute swim each morning before work soon developed into a love of the gym and taking care of herself. In two months she began to look healthier and her inner glow began to brighten.

At the gym she enrolled on an evening massage course to learn a new skill. Her male colleagues made saucy jokes about her choice of hobby, but it opened their eyes to her as a woman. No longer was she just one of the lads on the trading floor, she was a fit, sexy woman with everything going for her. Having so much male attention boosted her confidence, and she began to open up and even began to indulge in a little harmless flirting and banter.

Her male colleagues were green with envy when she took up with a gorgeous hunk from the gym, who had set up his own successful personal training business – so much so that many of them signed up as his clients!

Two years later they are still together and going from strength to strength.

Follow these Four Golden Keys and you'll unlock your inner goddess. You'll be that woman – the one who can choose just about any man she wants.

⁓ Part Three ⁓

CalcuDating

Part Three CalcuDating

If you're single, your number's up. My easy to follow CalcuDating System will change your approach to dating for the better in such a subtle way you won't even realise at first that you are changing direction. CalcuDating is utterly unique, and it's proven to work on even the toughest cases.

I devised my CalcuDating System four years ago, and I use it regularly on the clients who come to me for a Personal Dating Evaluation. It has been tried and tested and it works a treat.

Just like top therapies, including Cognitive Behaviour Therapy (CBT) or Neuro Linguistic Programming (NLP), the purpose of the CalcuDating System is to help you ditch old, negative behaviour patterns and learn to take a new positive, uplifting direction that will get you to where you want to be. Unlike some therapies that take weeks or months to kick in, by following the CalcuDating System you can begin benefiting from the LCFR programme from day one.

It was Isaac Newton's third law that every action had an equal and opposite reaction. Well, when it comes to love, this is the 'Lorraine Adams first law' – it's never truer in the art of finding a husband. How you look, the way you behave, how you interact with others – every little move you make will impact on your chances of finding a long-term partner. My goal is to work with you to maximise your positive behaviours and minimise those that others may find unattractive. I'm not trying to change you; I'm simply going to bring out the very best in you and discard the worst.

So, how does it work? It's easy – the CalcuDating System is a point-based 'love plan'. Every positive action, like smiling at a stranger or accepting a new date, earns you a score called a Match Point. However, every negative behaviour, such as obsessing over an ex, drunken dialling, or not making an effort with your appearance, docks your points. The CalcuDating System measures your good and bad behaviour patterns in uncomplicated, numerical terms that gauge your progress in a very black and white way. If you have the odd bad day, it's not all lost. You can cancel out your 'sins' by sticking to it and trying to recoup your lost points in other ways.

All you need to do is keep a weekly tally of your plus and minus Match Points, so we can assess your progress. Sooner than you realise, the upbeat stuff will start to become like second nature, and this will have a knock on positive effect. By repeating the good behaviours you will gain more and more self-assurance, and your confidence will be attractive and appealing to potential suitors. But I'll be honest with you, stage one, which is the first three months of the programme, is intensive – it is meant to be! You are changing bad behaviours of possibly a lifetime and shifting out of your comfort zone. Basically, if it's not hurting, it's not working. Doing well now will set you up for life and find you a lifetime partner. Not just someone who fits the bill for now, but someone who is right for you in more ways than you will recognise, in the first instances.

Teachers have long known that the best way to learn new skills is repetition – remember having your times tables drilled into you? At times you'll feel I'm repeating what you think you know, but I'll keep on at you until I believe it's become instinctive. Soon my CalcuDating System will be part of your daily routine. You won't even need to think about what to do; you'll be flirting and attracting the right men naturally. You will learn to stop fretting and agonising over unimportant trivial things. The fussing is usually the thing that holds you back from getting on the dating treadmill more than what you are actually fussing about!

One thing you need to come to terms with is that you cannot leap straight from single to couple – you need to go through the tentative stages of dating and embark on fledgling romances in order to lay the right foundations. Harville Hendrix Ph.D, *The New York Times* best-selling author, in his book *Keeping the love you find* reminds us about people who have 'fantasy world ideas about love'. Spending time ensuring you really understand what you want and need from a relationship, instead of skipping over it in the rush to get there quicker, will guide you to a union with staying power. As for the people you are dating, isn't it better they understand and discover the real non-artificial you, rather than being steam-rollered into getting to know an erroneous version of you?

My aim is to get you to a place where the right person finds you, rather than him feeling you're doing the chasing. I want to teach you to make the most out of every romance opportunity that comes your way, even if at first you don't recognise it as such. Sometimes I have clients who don't realise that the way they are behaving could be placing huge barriers along their path to finding love. Following the CalcuDating System makes everything more transparent; there will no longer be excuses for you to hide behind. When you start losing points, it will soon hit home what is working against you and you will begin to think twice before you fall back into bad habits.

So, how long does it take to get started? All my clients have to go through a three-month start up stage – stage one. If you collect near to maximum points during this stage, you will go directly to stage two at the end of the three months. You may, however, need a little more work, and that's fine. It's crucial to get this part right. There is no point you moving ahead if you are not ready, so if your Match Points score is low each month, you'll need to repeat stage one. Effectively, this means you could spend six months on the LCFR programme. I know it may seem like a long time but trust me, in the long term it will be far quicker than you making the same mistakes for the next ten years and still coming home alone every night.

The faster the CalcuDating System starts to resonate, the quicker you will be able to move to stage two – and romance opportunities will be coming your way more rapidly. The clients I have who become total disciples to the CalcuDating System, and who follow my LCFR programme to the letter, are the ones who fall in love and become part of a couple much sooner than those in denial. I have helped hundreds and hundreds of people to settle down with a loving partner; I know what I'm talking about. My advice is objective. I'm not your buddy or your sister, I'm your coach, and that's why I can get tough with you. I have no emotional attachment to you like your friends who advise you – they love you warts and all whereas I can tell it like it really is.

Getting started

Below is a table of the positive behaviours that I want you to start adopting. Maybe you already follow some of the suggested tasks, in which case it will be familiar and easy for you. If you are starting from scratch, don't worry; you will soon get into the swing of things.

Following the table of positive behaviours is the nasty 'negative behaviour' table, detailing the actions you really need to avoid. These are the passion killers that will lose you points, scare off every man in the neighbourhood and set you back weeks in your progress. Please photocopy the tables and add up your points on a weekly basis. (Or log on to www.CalcuDating.com and keep an online tally.) Later I will indicate how many points you need to reach each given week and month during your intensive three month plan.

It will be hard; you'll have to leave your comfort zone and you'll be pushed into a whole new way of looking at things. You will be taking a new, unfamiliar approach, but with the comfort of knowing my LCFR programme is tried and tested and will achieve a lot more for you in terms of romance than your efforts so far. So many women have accomplished happy unions by following my LCFR programme, and I've fixed up more marriages than anyone else I know, so you're hearing it from the best.

To make it a little easier for you, the LCFR programme is segmented into two busy, proactive months with a non-proactive month in the middle, when I won't be pushing you to accumulate quite so many points. Use your non-proactive month to kick back, not beat yourself up so much, and reflect on what you have achieved so far. By the time month three – your next proactive month comes around – you'll be raring to go again, with a renewed enthusiasm. It's easy to become complacent and feel you've not changed much when you have been on the plan for a few months, but you will be surprised at how much you have progressed. Before you embark on the LCFR programme you will write a few paragraphs in your dating diary (see Chapter one) about exactly how you feel, so you will be able to look back and remember just how bleak everything looked. You'll be surprised at how much more positive you've become over a short period of time.

The first three months of the LCFR programme could be the most important three months of your life – except those spent planning your wedding of course! If you work hard, you will find your life beginning to change. Men will start to show more interest, offers of dates will be coming your way, and your inner confidence will be blooming. It's my aim to build this 'virtuous circle' until you are the girl every guy wants to get to know. That may be hard for you to imagine right now, and I know it may all sound unachievable at this early stage, but believe me, I have seen countless women who had all but given up hope only to succeed in finding themselves in a beautiful relationship by simply following my programme.

OK – I hope you are clear about what you need to do, now let's get down to looking at the Match Point plan. I'm not going to shower you with points for every little smile at a stranger; you have to work hard at it to earn them.

Match point totals

- During the first proactive month, which lasts for five weeks, following the set tasks you can earn up to a total of 32 points.

- The next four weeks, month two, is the non-proactive month and you can earn a total of 16 points for tasks completed.

- On your third month, a proactive month lasting four weeks, you can earn a total of 28 points.

- Over the three months you can earn an extra 98 points if you accomplish the additional tasks set for you.

Match points positive behaviour table

There must be **absolutely no** cheating on points. You must complete every action in full to earn the Match Points otherwise you collect zero points. You are only conning yourself if you let yourself down and cheat! So, for example, on task one you must smile at 10 people or more to collect the two points awarded. If you only smile at five people on your 'smile' day you collect zero points.

Positive behaviour patterns	Points awarded	When to collect the points	Task number
Smiling at 10 strangers or someone you haven't spoken to or rarely speak to	2 points per completed task of 10 people	Collect total of 2 points once **every week** for whole three months	Task 1
Speaking to strangers after you've smiled at them (at least 2 per 'smile' day to gain maximum points)	2 points per completed task of 2 people	Collect total of 2 points once **every week** on your designated 'smile' day	Task 2
Starting a new interest or pursuit	2 points per completed task	Collect a total of 2 points on each of your proactive months	Task 3
Attending two events or social happenings to widen your network	2 points per completed task	Collect a total of 4 points per proactive month (two events)	Task 4
Going on a first date	2 points per completed task	Collect total of 6 points each proactive month	Task 5
Going on a successive date with someone you've already dated (but not an ex)	2 points per completed task	Collect a total of 6 points over the whole three months	Task 6
Additional tasks to earn extra points			
Joining a new online dating site	2 points for each new site	Collect a total of 4 points for the three months (for joining two sites)	Task 7
Communicating with at least two people on an online dating site	2 points per completed task of 2 people	Collect a total of 6 points for whole three months (2 people per month)	Task 8

Positive behaviour patterns	Points awarded	When to collect the points	Task number
Additional tasks to earn extra points			
Going on a date, even with someone you don't see as potential partner	2 points per person you date	Collect a total of 4 points each proactive month if two of the dates from Task 5 and/or 6 are with men you don't see as potential partners	Task 9
Spending five minutes three times a week on positive thinking visualisation	1 point for each completed week only	Collect a total of 13 points for whole three months	Task 10
Spending time accessorising your outfit 5 days out of every 7 days	1 point for each completed week only	Collect a total of 13 points for whole three months	Task 11
Putting some additional make-up on 5 days out of every 7 days	1 point for each completed week only	Collect a total of 13 points for whole three months	Task 12
Wearing something you feel dressed up in at least three times a week	1 point for each completed week only	Collect a total of 13 points for whole three months	Task 13
Paying someone a compliment, male or female, at least three times a week	1 point for each completed week only	Collect a total of 13 points for whole three months	Task 14
Doing at least 30 minutes of daily physical exercise at least five times a week	1 point for each completed week only	Collect a total of 13 points for whole three months	Task 15

Match Points negative behaviour table

Now look at the table of negative behaviour below. Every time you fall into one of these bad behaviours, you will accumulate points that will be deducted from your total.

Negative behaviour patterns	Points deducted
Rushing out of the house without putting any make-up on or with unkempt hair	1
Cancelling a date (Someone cancelling on you doesn't lose you points, but you cannot collect the points either.)	2
Instigating a phone call or sending a text or email to someone you've dated	2
Asking a guy how he feels about you or trying to extract his feelings and thoughts on you	2
Not attending a planned event, activity or social happening – unless you reschedule	2
Calling, texting or emailing an ex	1
Making negative comments about your status such as 'there are no nice men around' or 'all the best men are either gay or married'	1
Having too much to drink on a date – two glasses of wine is fine, two bottles isn't	1
Giving too much away about yourself on a first or a successive date	1
Becoming intimate (sexual) with someone on a first or second date – a little kissing is OK as long as it is brief	2
Turning down a date with someone for weak reasons such as age, height or profession	1

Match Points accumulator table

Use the following table to record your positive and negative points during the three months and then get out a calculator and tally them at the end. Alternatively, you can use the accumulator table on www.calcudating.com

Tasks	1	2	3	4	5	6	7	8	9	10	11	12	13	14	15	Total points deducted	Total points
Proactive month																	
Week 1																	
Week 2																	
Week 3																	
Week 4																	
Week 5																	
Total points																	
Non-proactive month																	
Week 6																	
Week 7																	
Week 8																	
Week 9																	
Total points																	
Proactive month																	
Week 10																	
Week 11																	
Week 12																	
Week 13																	
Total points																	

Example accumulator grid

Here is Lucy's Match Point accumulator grid, which is a typical example of how points can be earned (or lost) during the first month of the LCFR programme.

Tasks 1–6 are regular tasks	1	2	3	4	5	6	7	8	9	10	11	12	13	14	15	Total for regular tasks	Total for additional tasks
Week 1	2	2				2				1	1	1	1	1	1	4	8
Week 2	2	2	2	2				2		1	1	1	1	1		8	7
Week 3	2	2			2					1	1	1	1	1		6	5
Week 4	2	2								1	1	1	1	1		4	5
Week 5	2	2		2	2				2	1	1	1	1	1	1	8	8
Total points																**30**	**33**

- Completed all her Task 1 match points for 'smile' day, she also earned Task 2 points by communicating with the people she smiled at on 'smile' days.

- She started a new interest or pursuit in week 2 and earned total Task 3 points.

- She attended two events in week 2 and week 5 and earned total points for Task 4.

- On week 3 she went out on a date with someone she had dated previously so she earned two task 6 points there.

- In week 1 Lucy completed task 7 when she joined an online dating site and earned herself an additional 2 points.

- In week 2 she started to communicate with someone and earned two more points for Task 8.

- In week 5 she actually dated the man she had chatted to online even though initially she didn't really see him as a potential boyfriend which completed Tasks 5 and 9 and earned her four points in total even though it was just the one date.

- Lucy collected maximum points for task 10 by regularly doing her positive visualisation exercises.

- She earned maximum points for tasks 11, 12 and 13 by regularly taking pride in her appearance, also accessorising and making an effort with her make-up and hair.

- She gave out regular compliments to earn maximum points for task 14. Lucy only managed to complete Task 15 by doing regular exercise on weeks 1 and 5 so she didn't earn herself maximum points.

- Luckily Lucy didn't resort to ANY of the negative behaviour patterns, therefore had no points deducted. So all in all she did pretty well.

It may seem a lot to take in, but once you get going, it's simple. Remember the idea is to pace yourself; the last thing I want is for you to start to lose heart and give up because you are suffering from 'dating fatigue'. Think of the tortoise and the hare scenario. Running fast doesn't mean you'll win the race, and it certainly doesn't mean you'll be first up the aisle. Take it slow, get it right, and that ring on your finger is in sight.

With all the tools to hand, you are now ready to embark on the LCFR programme.

~ *Part Four* ~

Embarking on your life coaching for romance programme

Part Four Embarking on your life coaching for romance programme

You are about to embark on what could possibly be the most empowering journey of your life, the route to romantic bliss. In this section, we'll tackle the barriers that currently could be preventing you from finding lasting love, and we'll work together on some proven tactics and simple disciplines that will totally change your approach to dating and relationships so you can unearth the relationship success you have always dreamed about.

Before we begin, let's look at your love life so far. You may be someone who has been going through life armed with a wish list for your dream man. That's all well and good, but now I want you to consider also those slightly outside your wish list. In effect, I want you to give the guys you would normally dismiss a second look. At its most basic level, part of the LCFR programme is designed to open up your eyes and ensure you make the most of every romantic opportunity that comes your way. You've already read in this book the statistics that show four in five happy couples weren't instantly attracted to each other; so armed with that fact of life, I want to re-educate you to take a look at almost every man and to look deeper at what he has to offer. At first glance he may not seem like 'the one', however, he could have hidden qualities that didn't jump out at you the first time around. If you constantly remind yourself that not every mind-blowing love affair is going to sprout from someone who gives you goose bumps, then you'll be opening yourself to many more potential romance opportunities.

There may be other reasons you are failing to either recognise romance opportunities or to find the secret of sustaining a good relationship. In my decade-long experience of finding love for others, there are three types of woman who come to me – Blinkers, Freezers and the Rubber Rings.

Blinkers

Blinkers are by far the biggest group of single women. I find many women go through life totally blind – wearing 'blinkers'. They wouldn't recognise a romance opportunity if it got down on one knee and presented them with a fragrant bouquet of a dozen red roses. They are so busy looking for what they feel is their 'ideal' partner that they miss out on those men who are much more likely to be a better match. If you fall into this category, my job is to take off your 'blinkers' so you can properly consider *all* the opportunities placed before you.

Freezers

Single women who are Freezers are more open-minded and happy to consider dating a man who doesn't match their wish list, but they find it difficult to open up to any possibility of romance. Though they may like the look of a potential partner, when it comes to sending signals that they are up for a date, they 'freeze'. Men either can't read them or they find Freezers bland and move on swiftly. If this is you, don't panic. Parts of my LCFR programme will help you enormously with this dilemma. My aim is to get you to a place where being romanced and finding yourself the object of someone's affections begin to feel quite natural to you. I'll teach you how to go with the flow and surround yourself with men wanting more.

Rubber rings

And finally there are the single women who have no problem recognising romance opportunities, and certainly no problem opening up to them either, however, the Rubber Rings hit a huge hurdle sustaining a new relationship. They always fail to hang on to a man after the first few dates. Rubber rings are so desperate for a relationship that they'll grab onto the first man that comes along, practically grasping at anyone in the hope of diving into a relationship. They'll snatch out like they're drowning in a sea of singles – and a rubber ring is the only ring they're likely to get! Again, if you see a little of yourself here, don't worry. If you follow my advice, you will cruise through with ease and discover you can actually have a choice of eligible men. Instead of finding someone who nearly fits and hanging on for dear life because you don't want to be alone, you'll start to take your time with complete confidence. You will find that despite a ticking biological clock you will only allow yourself to settle with the right man, and not just someone who looks good on paper. Soon you could have your pick of men. Believe me this can and will happen, if you place your belief in my LCFR programme and throw your weight behind achieving top results.

But before you embark on my LCFR programme, you must be prepared for it mentally. Half-hearted attempts just won't work. Ask yourself: 'Do I really want to make changes in my life?', and tell yourself that you *can* make the change from being single to enjoying a happy relationship by exerting some positive effort. I have the tools and know how; I have the case histories; I have the proven track record: the only thing that needs to come from you is the effort. Don't make excuses to put off embarking on the LCFR programme – you can start it anytime

All you need to do is put your mind to it, get off your backside and go for it. I know the programme can be quite intensive, and if you are busy with a big project at work or trying to combat other downsides like weight loss or giving up smoking, then delaying for a few weeks may look like the most sensible option. However, before you do that, ask yourself honestly whether you are using delaying tactics. If the answer is yes, then put a bit of pressure on yourself to work hard – it will pay dividends in the long run. The sooner you start, the sooner you'll be on your way to enjoying life settled in a relationship. And having a holiday is no excuse – free time gives you more chances to put the plan into action.

Remember that I can't make it work for you – it requires your effort with a capital 'E'. I have the know-how and the tools, the tactics and track record, but the rest is up to you. Think of it just like a diet plan. If you cheat or take short cuts it will slow your progress, and the only one losing out is you.

Just to recap, as you can see from the CalcuDating System in Part three, stage one of the programme lasts for three months and is divided into three steps:

- Your first proactive month lasting five weeks

- Your second non-proactive month which lasts four weeks

- The third month which is proactive again lasting four weeks

If you accumulate enough CalcuDating Match Points during stage one you will progress to stage two. However, if after three months you haven't advanced enough, don't fret; it just means it is going to take a little longer for everything to really resonate. It is far better to get you right mentally, physically and emotionally, and feeling totally at ease with your new disciplines and tasks, before you start dating with proper relationship intent. Otherwise you are really just playing at it and getting nowhere fast. Many of my clients need longer for their new outlook and approach to set in.

If you need to repeat stage one of the LCFR programme, and try to earn more Match Points the second time around, that's OK. It's far better to have another three-month stab at it than wasting years in no-man's land, literally. If you follow the programme to the letter, it's *not* going to take you much longer to achieve the results. That's why the CalcuDating System is so superbly simple and clever; it makes you accountable to yourself.

You will swiftly see for yourself how earning the Match Points will bring you prizes – a noticeable change in your tactics will create a positive glow to your personality. If you're following the plan and racking up Match Points, then clearly things will be improving in your life. Knowing you're on such a great winning streak will boost your self-assurance to new levels, and this in itself will push you onwards and upwards.

Every new task and discipline has been carefully crafted to encourage a behaviour change. Psychologists have proven it's impossible to change a bad habit or leaning overnight, but when you keep on working at it over days and weeks, the negative tendencies fall away and the new, positive ones become second nature.

I know it's frustrating to take baby steps first, when you want to be out on dates looking for Mr Wonderful, but it's for your own good. I remember taking up boxing and training in a spit and sawdust boxing gym with my trainer as I wanted to get super fit. Ninety nine per cent of this gym's members were men, and all of them looked as though they could teach Mike Tyson a thing or two. Of course, I wanted to show off to the guys and start beating the punch bag. I turned up on day one with my shiny new gloves and professional grade skipping rope, but my trainer, a lovely bloke who went by the name of Jimmy Mac (a former British and European champion), shot me a withering look and insisted I spend at least six weeks on boring basic exercises. I was about to give up when two months in he finally let me loose on the boxing bag and speed ball. Because we'd spent so long getting the basics right, I could batter the bag looking like a pro-fighter. My stance, my footwork, it was all there; simply through repeating the step-by-step basics over and over again in the prep work. I left the gym that day with a huge smile on my face and some admiring glances from the guys training.

Following a week-by-week diary and breaking everything down into busy and quiet months, will stop you suffering from dating fatigue (see Chapter one). This will also take into account your feminine mood swings. The last thing I want to do is for you to go steaming ahead and end up becoming de-motivated. The time-scale of the LCFR programme is designed to help you stay on track more easily and gain the maximum points.

If at any stage of the programme you ever do feel like you can't stick with it, try positive thinking visualisations and mentally take yourself to the end result – you in a happy relationship (see Chapter eight). It usually does the trick. There is also a great self-hypnosis CD by Edgar Cayce you could listen too – I sometimes listen to if I get stressed (see page 167). Lose yourself in it for five or ten minutes and you will feel like a new woman.

The LCFR programme is just like a diet and requires the same kind of willpower. I'm sure you know friends who are forever starting new eating plans and diets, only to miss meals so they can have an extra glass of wine or helping of potatoes. The result is that they end up spending the next month moaning that they didn't lose any weight. In just the same way, if you drop parts of the programme because you find them uncomfortable, or fail to make up points in each area, you won't change all of your unhelpful behaviour patterns.

Stage one of the LCFR programme

The LCFR programme, and specifically the CalcuDating System, requires you to adopt new tasks and disciplines into your daily routine over the next 13-week period; each task and discipline is vital to your progress. Here is more information to help you on your path to finding that new dynamic you.

Tasks 1 and 2: first discipline — 'Smile Friday'

The first new discipline is what I call 'Smile Friday'. There's no particular need to do it on a Friday – you can choose any day of the week you like – but I like Fridays as people are generally in a good mood and looking forward to the weekend. Smile Friday is aimed at helping you to be become a more prolific communicator.

Communication is vital to making an impression on the opposite sex, but it's easy to forget this when we're wrapped up in our busy IPod and mobile phone induced everyday lives, which do make us somewhat insular. When you start practising 'Smile Friday' you'll realise how empowering it can be. Even if you are introvert and inhibited, you will quickly see what an effective tool a simple smile is for opening new romance opportunities.

For some people, smiling comes naturally. If you've been brought up in a close-knit community, smiling is as natural as breathing, but the city can make even the friendliest among us inwardly focused and shy away from making eye contact. I want you to step out of your comfort zone one day each week and make eye contact and smile. To earn your Match Points you will need to 'connect' with ten or more people every 'smile' day!

Smile Fridays can be simple once you start. Just take a deep breath before leaving your home in the morning, check your appearance and then make a conscious effort to make eye contact with whoever you meet on your daily routine. This means total strangers: people on the train, at the bus queue, in the supermarket, in the coffee shop. As soon as anyone returns your eye contact you smile. If people return your smile – and you will be surprised at how many do – progress to task two by saying hello or good morning or afternoon. If the thought leaves you filled with dread, to get used to it first try 'smile' day when you are with a friend.

Think how much friendlier you are on holiday abroad. You'll happily grin at fellow holidaymakers or inquisitive locals whom you've never met before. Grumpy looking old women and men break out into a beaming smile when you communicate with them, even if you can't speak their language. Why save this warm feeling for holidays when you can have it all the time at home?

It's amazingly empowering when you instigate warmth, and others return it to you. But make sure you vary the kind of people you smile at. It's not about winking at every fit man you pass! Instead, try smiling at old men and women, young men and women, attractive men and women, less attractive men and women. You need to smile and say hello to as many people as you can to collect your points. The only people you can ignore are strange looking or intimidating people, for obvious reasons. Don't try it late at night or in a secluded place – just stick to daylight hours or busy areas where you feel safe and secure.

When you get into a lift, don't gaze at the floor, fish inside your handbag or fiddle with your mobile phone. Instead, encourage yourself to make eye contact with the people already in the lift or who join you, and make light conversation. Simple phrases like 'lovely day' or 'Oh, nice tie' are fine – just say anything upbeat and kind that comes into your head. You'll be surprised at how easy it becomes. You'll also be surprised at how many conversations you start to have with complete strangers. Even more helpful is that you're building your skills to open a conversation with an attractive man, when perhaps in normal circumstances you would have spluttered and blushed bright red (or even gone out of your way to avoid him). After a few 'smile' days you'll find that light-hearted chit-chat comes quite naturally.

Smile Friday is a discipline that needs to be performed at least one day each week on both your proactive and non-proactive months. If you find it easy, and some of you will, you should practise Smile Friday as often as you can. If you find

Smile Friday tough and outside your comfort zone, work on doing it just once a week until you are used to it. When you become more comfortable communicating with strangers, then you can practise it more frequently.

The most attractive women are those who naturally engage with everyone around them, those for whom everyday is Smile Friday. With a little bit of work, being sunny soon becomes part of your personality.

Task 3: second discipline – your new pursuits and interests

The second discipline is one of the easiest tasks to get right, and will enrich your life in every single way. As we've already discovered together, one of the Golden Keys to unlocking your inner goddess is to be captivating and vibrant, with an aura of positive energy surrounding you. Following the second discipline will help you to achieve this, and make you feel like it comes naturally rather than forcing yourself to try and appear interesting to others.

All you need to do – and it really is this simple – is embark on new pursuits and interests. But do it with enthusiasm. We all know women who talk endlessly about starting a language course, or enrolling in a jewellery making or pottery class, but never get round to actually doing it. Compare these women to those who have started a new class and talk about it with sparkling eyes and excited tones. Now which one would you rather be and which one do you think attracts men like magnets? Making an effort to learn new skills and embrace new ideas is incredibly attractive.

Think back to when you were in your teens and early 20s. Life was a whirlwind with constantly changing ideas. You embraced every week with fresh tastes in food, clothes, music, fashion and even politics. However, when we reach our late 20s and progress into our 30s and 40s, we often start to stagnate a little. Set in our ways, we go to the same bars, the same restaurants and become, well – boring! To keep ourselves captivating, we must constantly evolve and take on new pursuits to keep that entrancing aura of infectious enthusiastic energy surrounding us.

You may be so busy with work that you may worry you won't have time to start new interests. What rubbish. If that's the case, how on earth will you find time for a boyfriend! If you want the LCFR programme to work, then you'll have to make time – it's for you, after all. For the second discipline, I want you to start *at least* one new interest or pursuit on each of your proactive months. It is often said that the busiest women are those likely to take on even more; it's the lethargic women who always make excuses and put things off who lose out. Men are not attracted to women who continually make excuses for not getting on and doing things.

Obviously you'll need to pace yourself and not go overboard. It may mean you change one class you currently attend for a new one, if time is a restraint. The aim is to try as many different interests as you can. Try and avoid insular or female dominated types of classes, such as yoga or swimming, although a female-only burlesque class is recommended, as you will gain a lot from it in other ways. You will meet far more men at a kayaking or rowing club, so think outside of the normal range of clubs you attend. Take a look at my suggestions later in this section for some other great ideas on where to meet men.

In addition to becoming more set in our ways in our late 20s and 30s, suddenly our social circle starts to shrink as well. Many friends couple up and get married; others are absorbed by work. We go out less often than we did in our teens and early 20s, so we naturally meet fewer new people. One of the key purposes of the second discipline is to start expanding your social network again – and I'm not talking about your Facebook friends. I mean real, live people you see and meet up with!

The key here is to increase the chances of meeting suitable single men. By the end of the first stage of the LCFR programme, I want you to have a fresh batch of interesting, like-minded people for you to network and socialise with. It doesn't take a maths genius to work out that love is a numbers game. The more men you meet, the greater your chances of meeting one you'll fall in love with.

Also, when you start to hang out with new people it's far easier to re-invent yourself a little. It can be tough to change you looks or style when you're stuck in the same social circle, but staying the same for years can come across as a bit bland and boring, and it has a detrimental effect on your personality. Spontaneity is the spice of life. Men love a spontaneous woman, and if it just isn't part of your make up you will be less appealing than a woman who has a bit of get up and go in her. Getting out of your comfort zone and starting a new interest, and changing your style and circle of friends, or at least adding to them, will do you the power of good and could bring out a whole subtle change in you that is so much more appealing than your old stable self.

Re-inventing yourself also allows you to change aspects of your personality that could be hindering your progress. Take the case of Aileen, a client who came to me as she found the only time anyone wanted to meet up with her was to pour out their woes. Aileen was a lovely, caring woman, and made a fabulous agony aunt – but really all she wanted to do was go out, let loose and have some fun. We worked together to get her started on some new pursuits, including a cookery class. When she found anyone gravitating towards her with his or her problems, she politely changed the subject and moved on. At first it was hard. She worried her new friends wouldn't want to know her if she didn't help them out, but she rapidly realised her new circle saw her as someone fun, not a dumping ground for their upsets and issues. In turn, this made her more confident in dealing with her family and old friends – and meant she gained a far more satisfying social life.

Trying new pursuits will up your energy, increase your aura of attraction and give you plenty to talk about with every new man you meet. Here are some ideas to get you started, but feel free to try anything new that appeals to you. I've also listed a few pursuits to avoid, as they are more often attended by women and not men.

Pursuits to try:

- Running club
- Motor mechanics
- Garden design and maintenance
- Photography
- Graphic design
- Creative writing
- Cookery
- Wine appreciation
- Computing
- Music
- Philosophy
- Languages
- Sailing, kayaking and rowing clubs
- Animation classes
- Politics lectures and debates
- Boxing gyms
- Sports massage
- Spin class
- Dance classes

Pursuits to avoid:

- Yoga
- Fashion design or dressmaking
- Jewellery design
- Interior design
- Swimming lessons

What your second discipline will help you achieve

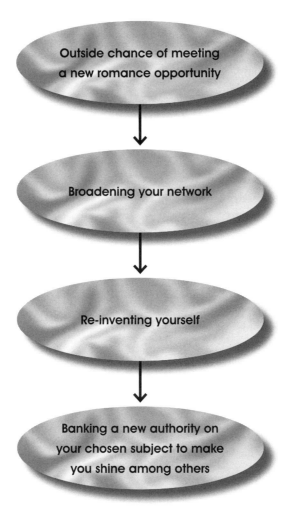

Outside chance of meeting a new romance opportunity

↓

Broadening your network

↓

Re-inventing yourself

↓

Banking a new authority on your chosen subject to make you shine among others

Task 4: third discipline — new monthly networking events

Just like the second discipline, the third new discipline is all about meeting more new people. You need to follow the third discipline on your proactive months. Quite simply, I want you to attend two or three new social events each month, with the aim of broadening your circle of friends. I don't want or expect you to go alone, so don't panic.

You may think the quickest way to broaden your social circle is in bars or clubs, but I discourage this. What was a great hunting ground in your teens and early

20s won't work as well as you get older (and the men you meet in nightclubs won't be the marrying kind). Nor do I want you hanging out at singles events. This may seem very strange coming from me – the lady who introduced speed dating to the UK – but I'll explain why. I've run plenty of singles nights in my life, but they are now so ubiquitous that in many cases it's about quantity not quality. There may be dozens of men there, but like at bars and clubs, possibly not always the sort you'd want to meet.

Instead, I'd like to see you try more upmarket and interesting social events. You can still scout for single men, but you won't appear in any way desperate. Try meetings like art launches, book signings, lectures and debates. Look at my list on page 76 for some fresh ideas. The great thing about these types of events is that you can trot along with anyone, your sister, your married or loved-up pals, your gay best friend, even an ex – you don't have to rock up alone.

I've found the best results come from when couples meet at a less-obvious event than a singles night. The atmosphere is more relaxed and there isn't an underlying agenda to every conversation. However, if you feel you need a little banter and flirting practice, then attending a singles night with a single friend might be helpful; just don't build up your hopes that you're about to meet a future husband. Instead, use it as a chance to try out your new-found smile power and to chat with men and move outside of your comfort zone.

You may ask me what's the point of going out if you may only meet people who are in a relationship, but what I think you'll find is that at most social events there will be a mix of people. If you find yourself attracted to someone who then reveals he has a partner, don't worry. Just use your time talking with him to build your conversation and banter skills. There's no such thing as a lost opportunity – every interaction will benefit you in lots of ways.

Whereas singles events sometimes feel a little too contrived, meeting in a less pressured environment means you can take more time to get to know men who interest you. This will lay a solid foundation for any future relationship. I appreciate it may make it more difficult to spot opportunities for romance – some men will be in couples, others may be gay – but it's a more natural way to meet. This exercise is really all about improving your social skills as much as anything else. It's the part of my LCFR programme that will prepare you for when you start to attract those men you find appealing. Here are some superb ideas to get you started.

Community clear-ups An American idea where the whole neighbourhood gets together to tidy up green spaces or local streets. Increasingly popular in the UK, they won't win any prizes for glamour but are a marvellous way to meet the hottest men living close to you and they show you're caring too.

Dog walking Meeting men can be a stroll in the park. Offer to walk a neighbour's pooch and you'll instantly get chatting to other dog owners. Men with pets are generally fitter and more likely to settle down than those without.

Gallery openings Free wine and instant conversation, as you have to talk about the art on show. Galleries openings are great informal get-togethers and you can drop in even if you only have half an hour to spare.

Big Lunch A new scheme to get neighbours together for a communal lunch. Each person brings a dish they cooked. Organise one in your area or keep an eye out in the local press for the nearest one to you.

Open house and garden events Learn about Britain's most beautiful buildings and homes, and if you are particularly interested in architecture what better way to meet like-minded men. These types of events are favoured by architects, creative types and men who are looking to buy their own homes.

Book signings Get yourself on the mailing list of publishers and book shops such as Hatchards. They will email you and let you know when there is an event in your area and which book and author will be presented.

Guerrilla Dining Pop-up restaurants are a new trend where cooks whip up wonderful meals in their own homes and invite strangers to pay just like a restaurant.

Marketing focus groups Focus groups pay up to £75 for your opinion on a new brand or advertising campaign. You spend up to three hours together with a group of ten to 12 others, and if you like someone, there's plenty of chance to chat.

Citysocialising.com A new website for people to make friends with others into the same activities. Activities range from art galleries to watching Twilight films, and it operates in 50 British towns and cities.

Lectures Choose a course with a weekly meeting for at least a month, which gives you time to form bonds with your fellow students. At the end of the lecture, suggest to those you meet you all go to a bar or coffee shop to carry on the conversation and catch the eye of anyone you'd like to get to know better.

For more information on event ideas or suggestions about new interests and pursuits go to www.calcudating.com

Tasks 5–9: fourth discipline – more regular dating

The fourth discipline is quite simply – date much more often. You must aim for a target of two to three dates per proactive month. If the thought of so many dates fills you with fear, you can relax; the other disciplines will help you, and I have countless clever tricks you can use to find you plenty of great dates.

The key to completing this particular task successfully is not to focus solely on those men you immediately see as potential partners. Instead, you must **learn to accept dates from men you wouldn't necessarily consider a prospective boyfriend.** This task is vital. If you start opening your heart and mind to unlikely men, you'll progress far faster towards meeting 'the one'.

In my experience, every man you believe is a Mr Not-Quite-Right should come with a big sign: Warning! Do Not Over-Look; Could Be Mr Right. You're not seeing these men for what they are and giving them a second glance (or even a first glance), as you're so hung up on finding your mind's ideal picture-perfect man. But they could have something very special that you just don't pick up on initially.

I'm not suggesting you 'settle' for second best or that you forget your dream of falling hopelessly in love. I'm simply asking you to explore every opportunity and to open your eyes wider, without any limiting or preconceived ideas about the person. Instead of seeing men in just two categories – boyfriend material and non-boyfriend material – there's a middle ground, and it's usually here you'll find your Mr Right. I know at this point you may not be convinced, but all I can tell you is that the majority of successful matches I have made have developed from two people who did not initially give each other goose bumps.

Remember how I told you about how I met my late fiancée? I wouldn't have given him a second glance if I'd met him on a night out. He was older, overweight and had the most dreadful dress sense, but when I got to know him, I realised what an amazing, entertaining, charismatic person he was. If you told me after our first meeting that I would fall madly in love with him, I would have bet you a million pounds it wouldn't happen. Although I found him fascinating and interesting, I could not bring myself to find him physically attractive. Even kissing him would have repulsed me in those early days.

However, as we saw each other more frequently, and as we chatted over the telephone, I felt more and more drawn to him. Suddenly his bad taste in clothes, his balding 'comb over' hairstyle, the fact he was grossly overweight, all melted away and became unimportant. I became excited by his mind and the way he carried himself; his gestures, his drive and ambition. We fell deeply in love, and once we'd consummated the relationship, I set about sorting out that dodgy wardrobe and getting him on a diet!

So believe me when I say it's not just talk. I've walked the path before you, and I've seen countless people walk the same route out of singledom.

Another point to remember is that dating men you don't quite fancy also helps build your flirting skills. It aids your understanding of the banter between men and women in a fledgling relationship, and will help you feel more comfortable on a 'date' situation. Try it and see for yourself how much more relaxed you become on a date.

First dates

Don't put yourself under too much pressure. There's nothing worse than planning an expensive meal followed by a bar or club. First dates should always be 'coffee only' and you must avoid alcohol at all costs. A first date should just be a 'taster' to allow you to get a feel of what type of person he is. Also, set a maximum time limit of two hours. You can always arrange to see each other for longer next time.

If after the first date you decide he's boring, irritating or intimidating, then don't feel pressured into meeting him again. However, if you had fun but don't fancy him, give him another chance at suggesting another date; give him your number and see what happens.

Second dates

A woman should **never** instigate a second date, whether she fancies him or not. In fact a woman should never instigate a further date even if she has dated the guy several times. Always leave this in the hands of the guy so he has to chase you. I know it's an age-old rule – but it is the best rule. Successful dating, which progresses rapidly into a good, stable relationship, will usually only come by abiding by this 'rule'.

Of course, you can give him a clue that you are willing to meet again. Lines that work include: 'Well I really must go, but it has been interesting/lovely to meet you. Drop me a line or give me a call if you want to meet again.' But **never** push for a time, date and location. Always allow the man to do this, either during the date or at a later stage. Remember a man loves a feminine woman, and leaving the man to decide when he is meeting you again is a wily feminine trait they find very appealing. You can read more about posing yourself a challenge and learning the most appealing womanly arts in later chapters.

After the date

As I've mentioned before, **never** follow up a date with a text or call to say 'thank you, nice meeting you' or anything else. This leaves no room for the man to pursue you. Trust your belief in yourself and that you're a catch. If you project this, he'll pick up on it. If he has any sense he'll pursue you, but if he doesn't, you chasing him isn't going to instigate him suddenly falling at your feet. If none of your dates want to see you again – even the ones you find dull – then you have to go back to the drawing board. See Part one: Tough love – your self-evaluation.

If you find you are simply not able to find anyone to date, then you will find the chapter on the 'world wide wed' extremely helpful. I am not guaranteeing that you will find the love of your life immediately from an online dating site, but it will certainly aid you in your search and it will definitely give you plenty of practice.

Task 10: fifth discipline – positive thinking and visualisation

This task is about how positive thinking and practising positive thinking visualisations can help you refocus when you are finding things a little tough. The last thing I want you to do is to give up on the LCFR programme or to weaken when it comes to some of the tasks, so if you are starting to waiver remember positive thinking. Read more about this is in later chapters.

Tasks 11 to 13: sixth discipline — looking your best

These three tasks are more about the way you present yourself. Many women tell themselves the right man will see through the visual aspects of a woman and will be more interested in her personality. The truth is he will be more likely to find the drive to invest time into finding out more about your 'inner beauty' if he is helped along the way by someone who is pleasing on the eye. Also, when you read about rediscovering your feminine womanly charms in Chapter five you will understand that there is even more to a woman than her personality and looks.

Applying yourself to discipline six will also have a huge impact on your self-esteem. When people pass comment and you have extra glances, it will undoubtedly make you feel better and more positive about yourself giving you more of a bounce in your step, This will undoubtedly get picked up on.

Task 14: seventh discipline — compliment others

Paying others compliments will give you as much pleasure as it will give them. The warmth and good feeling this generates is worth the few seconds it takes to divert your attention from whatever you are doing and tell someone they look well, their hair looks lovely or that you love their new tie. Give compliments freely to both men and women. I am a true believer in good Karma, and it's never let me down yet.

Task 15: eighth discipline — exercise regularly

Exercise is one of the great freebies in life, so no excuses; you don't have to pay for an expensive gym membership to do this task. Think of regular exercise as your regular feel good booster, releasing those happy endorphins into your brain. It beats drink, drugs, cream cakes or cigarettes! You undoubtedly look and feel better through regular exercise, and this is why it is a vital part of my LCFR programme.

Stage one summary

At the end of the 13-week intensive LCFR programme you will have completed stage one, mastered eight new disciplines and successfully completed the 15 tasks, and hopefully you will be confident and ready to move onto stage two. To do this you will need a score sheet with total Match Points within the following ranges.

Month 1: (Proactive)
A total of 26 to 32 Match Points for your monthly tasks

Month 2: (Non proactive)
A total of 12 to 16 Match Points for your monthly tasks

Month 3: (Proactive)
A total of 24 to 28 Match Points for your monthly tasks

Points for additional tasks
A total of 92 to 98 Match Points for your additional tasks and disciplines

---

If you reach the required scores well done! You can move to stage two, but before you do, you will need to look back in your mood diary and add your feelings now that you're ready for stage two. If, however, you are nowhere near the required scoring levels, the best favour you can do yourself is to keep at it and continue on a month on—month off basis until the new tasks and disciplines become easy for you to achieve. I suggest a further three months.

Stage two of LCFR programme

The second stage of my LCFR programme, assumes that you are now dating more regularly and that men are pursuing you, and is all about you keeping up the great new disciplines you've learned. You may think it is exceeding optimistic that after just three months you are regularly going on dates, but that's how positive I am that this programme can change your life for the better. I've seen it work thousands of times, on all types of women, and if you follow it correctly it **will** work on you.

I'm not going to presume that after three months intensive work on yourself that you are holding hands with the love of your life – but hey it could happen! Most of you **will**, at the very least, be in a completely different space emotionally and have a more cheerful and upbeat outlook. If things have not yet started work-ing as well as you hoped after spending three months on the LCFR programme, and you still feel romance isn't coming your way, don't give up. Go back and give stage one of the programme a little more time. All of us are at different stages, and some of us need to feel comfortable with the new approach for it to start taking effect. Persevere for a further three months and you **will** get there.

If you are starting to feel more attractive and are receiving the right feedback – well done! You'll soon find it becomes a 'virtuous circle' with each good date making you feel even more gorgeous. Soon you'll have a large circle of admirers all vying for your attention. I hope that after three months on the LCFR programme, your new disciplines have become second nature and an integral part of your everyday life.

- If you look forward to Smile Friday and find you are making eye contact and communicating with random people more regularly – it is working.

- If you are dating every week, meeting new people and keeping an open mind to every man you meet – then you have come a very long way in the right direction.

- If you have so much more going on in your life and you are expanding your social group – you are nearly there.

However, be warned. For stage two to work you need to ensure you:

- Don't become complacent and slump back into your old habits.

- Don't feel deflated that you haven't met your soul mate already.
  He will come, I promise you; just stick with it and be patient.

Day by day try to keep improving yourself. Think of the LCFR programme like an amazing diet that has lost you a stone in weight. Those who become complacent, sneaking in bread with dinner or a few extra glasses of wine, pile the pounds back on; but those who keep going can add slinky dresses to their wardrobe, get more attention from men, are physically and mentally healthier and feel happier about themselves.

Dating more regularly will introduce you to lots more different types of men, and it will help you to understand them better: the way they think, feel, act, react and go about things. It will help you to understand what type of man you are more suited to, and you will no longer waste time going blindly into relationships with men you think you are attracted to. In my extensive experience, I've identified four types of men, each type has appeal and downside.

The Dependables
✓ Dependables will adore you.
✓ They are thoroughly modern metro sexual men who help around the house.
✓ They will buy you gifts, however, these are more likely to be something practical rather than romantic.
✓ Dependables will rarely stray and will often forgive you for an infidelity; they are incredibly loyal.
✗ Dependables can be ever so slightly dull. These aren't men to send shivers down your spine or make you go weak at the knees.
✗ They can be money conscious and picky about who pays for what.
✗ Dependables will not be highly driven or ambitious but can hold down great well-paid, high-powered jobs.

The Lady-killers

✓ Lady-killers always look good and draw admiring glances

✓ They are very masculine

✓ They will always pay for every single thing and want to treat you like a queen

✓ They will usually be at the top of their field, whatever business they are in

✓ Lady-killers will make your heart flutter every time their name flashes up on your phone screen

✗ Lady-killers are natural born flirts and try it on with every other woman; you will never feel secure

✗ They are not terribly sensitive to your needs and won't play a particularly supportive role in your life

✗ They will not tolerate you getting out of shape or not looking your best

✗ They are selfish and self-centred; it's all about them, not you

✗ Lady-killers won't tolerate you flirting with other men

The Players

✓ A Player will always take you to the best places; he's adored by everyone he meets

✓ He will spoil you rotten with lavish gifts and love to take you shopping

✓ He will be amazing in bed and make you feel like a sensuous woman

✓ A Player will be fascinating, intriguing and usually have a sparkling sense of humour

✗ A Player will always have other women in his life

✗ He will be secretive and frequently go missing or silent on you

✗ He will expect a lot from you emotionally and expect you to be 100% supportive

✗ A Player usually has a deep-seated insecurity about himself and will need you constantly brushing his ego

The Chump

✓ There are plenty of them to choose from!

✓ You won't ever have to worry about him straying

✓ He will do anything you say

✗ He'll frequently get irritable, but will never tell you why or hold open discussions with you — he hates any form of confrontation

✗ He often looks a mess (but he is easy to restyle and very open to your help)

✗ You will always have to pay your way

✗ The Chump won't be ambitious and couldn't care less about making it to the top of his chosen career

Looking through the list, you'll probably say you want a man who is a combination of the best bits with none of the negative aspects. Don't we all! My advice to you is to wake up and join the real world. Once any man hits his 30s, it's highly unlikely he'll ever change his ways – and **all** men will fall into one of these four types.

Now I don't want you to feel down about this. My aim isn't for you to give up on men completely. I told you when we began this journey together that I'm known for my honesty, and I've been on the dating scene long enough to know the way men work, think and act.

It may be you haven't been lucky in love so far because you've been searching for a dream date with all of the ups and none of the downs. Now that you know he doesn't exist, you can either start your search without the rose-tinted glasses and find yourself a real living, breathing man, or you can close this book and go back to your 'leaving it to fate', fantasy-land attitude.

If you are still reading, and accept that whoever you date will fall into one of the four types, whichever one it is, there are some wonderful positives to enjoy and embrace. If you want the spine-tingling melting moments; if you want him to look great; and if he pays for everything and treats you like a queen, then you are going to have to accept that he may stray, or at least flirt. He will leave you feeling insecure and he isn't going to be the most supportive or understanding partner. Learn to manage your expectations, and indeed manage and 'man-ipulate' your man, and then the drawbacks won't be so difficult to deal with.

Remember, life isn't like the movies. No man you meet will ever be the best of everything you see on the big screen. You won't be whisked away to Paris every weekend or come home to a house filled with candles and red roses. It's more likely you put your key in the door to find him snoring on the sofa, having left a trail of mud on the carpet from his dirty football boots and the loo seat up. That's real life – and if you embrace it and accept it, you'll also find real love.

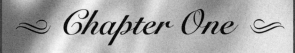

∽ *Chapter One* ∽

Your personal dating diary

Chapter One Your personal dating diary

Now you've discovered the skills for finding lasting love, it's time to put them into practice. To get the most from your LCFR programme, you need to be focused and organised, and the best way to do this is with a diary. Don't leave arranging dates or trying new interests until the last week of the month, as you'll feel flustered and pushed for time. Instead, space each date, new pursuit and social event out evenly throughout the month to make the most of every new opportunity. You'll also need to keep a personal diary, so you can keep a record of your progress – and hopefully congratulate yourself on how far you've come.

Your dating diary

Just like a gym programme, your dating diary will keep you on track, telling you what you need to do and when. Remember, if you work hard you could complete stage one of the programme within just three months, and your life could change for the better that quickly. But if you're disorganised or lazy, and don't pre-plan each and every activity, the programme will take longer. The choice is yours – you know what you need to do!

To help you plan and manage your three-month LCFR programme go to www. coffeeandcompany.com, where you can get your login to the dating diary and you will find lots of suggested events, pursuits and reminders of how to keep on track. Also look online or in the local newspaper for inspiration. If you prefer, you could create your own calendar with a similar PC application.

Each month enter in your diary your tasks and disciplines, to help you stay on track. The earlier you organise yourself, the more Match Points you will earn, and the closer you will be to finding your ideal man.

Your personal diary

Alongside your dating diary, it's also important to keep a diary of your thoughts and feelings. When you start out, write down how you're feeling now and what you are hoping to achieve. At the end of each month write down how you feel as a result of following the programme. It's also important to record your thoughts on your progress at the end of the intensive 13 weeks that make up stage one, before moving on to stage two.

Keeping a personal diary is important. It is great to look back and see how far you have come. I'm almost certain you will forget just how bad things were, and therefore you might not realise how much you've achieved. Your diary will keep you in touch with reality.

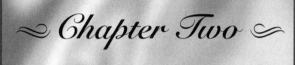

Chapter Two

The world wide wed

Chapter Two The world wide wed

Internet dating can be one of the most effective and rewarding adventures when looking for love. But it can also be a demoralising experience that will leave you thinking there's no hope. Recent statistics show that six in ten singles have turned to the net to find love, and cyber dating *is* amazingly successful. A quarter of all newlyweds now find their partner online, and 94 per cent of people meeting up through websites go on to a second date.

But on your journey to meeting Mr Right online, it's worth remembering you'll meet many Mr Wrongs along the way. Some men will only be looking for sex – but that's the same as the offline world; others may be looking for genuine love, but it may not be with you.

Internet dating is different to meeting men more traditionally, simply because it makes things easier. When men and women are faced with the huge choice of partners you can find online, you may find they forget their manners. Their profile may read like a Mills and Boon character, but if on meeting you turn out to be not their type, it's easy to feel hurt when they stop responding to your online messages and emails.

Too many times I've seen women devastated because they've been rejected in cyberspace. I've had female clients protesting that 'all men are the same' or 'men are only after one thing' when it is simply not true. Remember it's difficult for men too – and guys get a bad press. Men tell me that whatever they do, women say it's the wrong thing. If a man meets a woman online and then finds he's not attracted to her, it makes things awkward for him. If he tells her straight, she will say he is commitment phobic. If he avoids her later online, she'll complain he's a game player or womaniser. If he comes up with an excuse about his ex or not being ready for a relationship, to avoid hurting her feelings, then she'll attack him for being a timewaster. It is nearly impossible for a woman to accept that she just doesn't appeal to him – for whatever reason.

Men on the other hand can accept this more easily and take rejection far better. A man rarely lashes out at a woman he doesn't fancy. He is unlikely to accuse her of being commitment phobic or a time waster. He'll just get up, dust himself down and move on to the next one. Women seem to have far more false pride and take every rejection as a personal slight. I believe we have a lot to learn from men on how to behave here.

So be prepared for some rejections. Online dating is a numbers game, and you need to accept that you won't appeal to everyone out there. There are six million Brits currently signed up for online dating sites, so while not all of them will be right for you, some of them certainly will.

To gain the best from online dating you need to be armed with the right tools and know how. There are five main areas of online dating you need to understand:

Choosing your site

Most people starting to look for love online will automatically go for one of the giant international sites they've seen advertised on TV or in other media. While you'll certainly have a huge amount of profiles to trawl though, ask yourself honestly if you'll have much in common with any of them? I liken finding the right site to choosing a night out. Most average Joes or Joannas will be happy to choose a loud chain pub; it won't be anything special but there will be loads of people there. However, someone with more refined tastes and interests will look for somewhere more interesting and individual. And those with more cash to splash will select an exclusive venue where they want to be seen. So, deciding on which online dating site you are going to try is very similar. Make sure you pick one that reflects your personality; that way you're much more likely to find your kind of men.

Most sites will allow you to register and look through profiles for free – you only pay when you want to get in touch with someone. It's well worth doing your homework and looking through lots of sites to assess the quality of each site's members. Look up key words and phrases on internet search engines – for example 'exclusive dating', 'sporty dates', 'dating for single parents' or 'dating for the over 50s'. There are hundreds of sites to choose from and three or four will be right for you.

You'll quickly realise the huge generic sites come up in almost all your searches. This is because they have a multi-million pound marketing and advertising budget and throw cash at luring in new members. But if you scroll down the list of choices you'll start to find the more interesting niche sites that may well offer better opportunities.

Most Internet dating site fees range from around £15 to £50 per month. The fee doesn't always reflect the calibre of people or even the number of members on offer. Joining the site usually becomes cheaper the more months you sign up for – but this isn't always a good idea. There's no point tying yourself into a three- or six-month membership if after just a week you realise the men on the site aren't for you; it's more effective to try the one-month option first. This way you can try three or four different sites over a few months, rather than being stuck with one for months on end.

If you're looking for inspiration, in Appendix two I have put together a list of recommended sites, each with a brief description of the market they are reaching for. These are sites I know, trust and recommend to my clients, and the list demonstrates the sheer range of people internet dating caters for.

Your profile

Your profile is your advert to the world and it's vital you get it right. You are marketing your charms and all you have to offer; it's your chance to catch a guy's eye before he moves on to the next girl. So why are so many profiles absolutely awful?

Spend just half an hour online and you'll quickly realise that most people's profiles read more or less the same. Women will write 'I'm just as happy on a night out on the town with friends as I am curled up on the couch with a good DVD'. Most of the men's profiles will include a line about this being the first time they have done anything like this. Even the serial daters! Men also attempt to impress by boosting their salary, height and sporting interests, while women play down their extra pounds and knock a few years off their age.

Most men in their late 30s and early 40s rule out women in the same age group in their online searches, so if you fall into this category it may be more fruitful to omit your age. OK, so it's a white lie, but at least it gets your profile in front of him for consideration.

One of the worst mistakes online daters make is listing everything and anything about themselves in their profile. Remember the purpose of the profile is to intrigue and get someone hooked on you so they want to make contact and find out more – it's not a job application or a CV for your entire life. A profile doesn't have to be long-winded. Most dating sites offer a separate section where you can list your likes and dislikes and your interests and hobbies, so leave this information until later.

Before writing your profile, take a look at the ones you like. See what catches your eye, what makes you laugh, and why you'd want to contact that person. Make sure your profile is original and avoid all the clichés that other women use. You need to stand out, not blend into the background. My best advice is to avoid talking about yourself and what you are looking for in a partner. And remember the point of a profile isn't to impress – it's simply to entice someone to find out more about you. Don't boast or try to show off; instead try to inject some humour. One of the best profiles I have ever seen was a self-depreciating list of the writer's worst qualities. It read:

'Well, I'm the wrong side of 35 and have seen better days. I'm thinning on top and no, you wouldn't mistake me for Brad Pit, even at 50 paces. I'm grumpy in the mornings and sometimes in the afternoon, but rarely in the evenings with a chilled glass of wine in my hand. I make enough money but spend far too much — and I'm stuck in my ways with some bloody annoying habits. If you want Mr Perfect, you'd better move on to the next profile.'

The profile was hilarious, but at the same time intriguing. Any woman reading it could never be quite sure if it was serious or written in jest. But it did attract more interest and comments than any other profile I have come across – and I bet he was inundated with dozens of dates.

Another great way to enthuse people to want to find out more about you is to compare yourself to a car, or animal or even a country. Or try borrowing the traits of several well-known celebrities – good and bad. The most interesting pro-files are ones that include fun and a feeling that the writer is enjoying himself or herself. Many are tongue-in-cheek, which indicates the person behind the profile isn't desperate for a date. Those of us who don't take ourselves too seriously are often the most genuine and interesting. Don't fall into the line of thinking that if a profile isn't serious the person writing it isn't looking for a serious relationship; noth-ing could be further from the truth.

If you're really lost for words, ask a friend for help. You can even pay a professional profile writer. And if you're finding talking about yourself in cyberspace tough, I'm worried you may struggle on a real date, so you may find it helpful to review the information in previous chapters to boost your confidence both online and off.

The photo(s)

First impressions count – and nowhere more so than in online dating. Profiles with photos are viewed five times more often that those without, so it's essential to include one.

Like profile writing, it's another area where many singles don't put enough thought and effort in. An amateur snap you've taken by holding the camera at arm's length is only going to interest men so desperate they will meet anyone. The best pictures are holiday photos taken when you felt at your best and look relaxed and happy. You'll radiate happiness and this will catch the eye of anyone flicking through a string of profile pictures.

Shots taken when you were unaware or not posed usually look good as do 'action' photos, as long as you avoid putting up photos where you are just a dot on the horizon. It's fine to include skiing or paragliding shots, for example, as it does show other sides to your personality, but only if you also include a close up of your face. It is also best to remember less is more – especially if you are not particularly photogenic. One average looking snap is better that a lot of them.

If you don't have a recent photo you like, you can include shots up to two or three years old providing your haven't changed your appearance. But don't cheat and upload ones where you were several kilos lighter. This is false advertising and men will run a mile when they meet you.

I often recommend getting profile photos done professionally. It doesn't cost too much if you shop around, and you can lower the price by selecting one or two of the best pictures rather than buying the whole photo shoot.

Effective communication

The best sites are those that allow you to send a quick flirt or 'wink' to the people who you find the most appealing. While normally I don't advocate women making the first approach, online the rules are different. In cyberspace men tend to sit back and wait for women to give them a signal before they make an approach, so the quick flirt makes it easy for men to see you are interested.

Once you've found a handful of profiles you like the look of, send a quick flirt. Most sites have a readymade message such as 'I like the look of your profile what do you think of mine?' Send out as many as you like to profiles on your hit list, then simply wait for the response.

If you have a great photo and an interesting profile, the majority of the men you target will reply. However, when he responds the secret is to keep it brief. Be intriguing and don't give too much away. Remember the man will want to chase you and he will only pursue you if he finds you challenging. Don't respond to the messages immediately – leave it a day, or even two, but no longer.

The best method for online dating is to allocate three or four 30-minute sessions a week for searching, sending quick flirts, responding and arranging to meet. Don't spend more time on it and don't be tempted to check your inbox every few hours.

Keep your communication short and sweet, and include a little light-hearted banter. Never come across as too willing, even if you sent him the first communication. Take your time to respond and don't pour out your life history in the first few messages. Also, don't get drawn into long-winded online chats. Men who do this are time wasters and the sort of guys who have no interests other than chatting online. Many of them are already in relationships and use the online world as a means of fantasy escape.

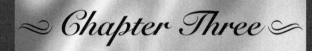

~ Chapter Three ~

Men versus women:
the battle of the sexes

Chapter Three Men versus women: the battle of the sexes

In this chapter, I will give you some tips about men and an insight into how their behaviour and thinking differs so much from women. My aim is to help you avoid misconstruing your date's actions, and in doing so, throwing away another potentially good romance unnecessarily.

The fundamental differences between men and women

Every woman knows how difficult it is to understand men – but why is it? Quite simply, it's because we think so differently. We've evolved to be different and to carry out different roles in life. No matter how sophisticated your lifestyle is, there's no getting away from the fact that men are the hunters and women are the nurturers. Women are adept at juggling tasks, caring for children, getting on with big groups of people, and remembering everything that's needed to run a household. Do you know a single man who can do all that and with a smile on his face?

Men on the other hand are great at concentrating on *one job at a time only* and getting it done, and it's this that causes more heartbreak to women that any other aspect of male behaviour. Scientific studies show men can only effectively carry out one task at a time, so if he's at work, with his friends, playing sports or driving his car, it's unlikely he'll be thinking about you or contacting you. It doesn't mean he doesn't care; his mind is just elsewhere.

A woman can spend all day thinking about a new love prospect, but also go to work, complete the shopping, call her mum, meet her best friend for a coffee *and* get a blow dry. The net result? You've spent ten hours pining over him, while he's thought of you for perhaps half an hour, top whack. It doesn't necessarily mean the relationship is unequal. He is quite simply a man and you are a woman.

It is well worth remembering that women spend three times longer than men talking and expressing their emotions. Men on the other hand are wired to compartmentalise everything in their lives. They don't do cosy 'feelings' chats – and you shouldn't be offended by this.

A man segments his mind into separate compartments for every part of their world: you, work, family, friends, hobbies, sex and everything else he's interested in.

While we can dip into all (or most) of these at once, he needs to close up one box before opening another. And if you don't believe me, listen to the words of renowned psychologist Dr Luann Brizendine, author of *The Female Brain*. She wisely says, 'Women have an eight-lane superhighway for processing emotion, while men have a small country road.' She adds, 'I believe women actually perceive the world differently from men. If women attend to those differences they can make better decisions about how to manage their lives.' (Brizendine, Dr L, 2006, *The Female Brain*. Morgan Road Books. ISBN 0-7679-2009-0.)

In other words, what you may perceive as a problem in the relationship, or a sign that he doesn't like you, is nothing of the sort. It's just a man being a man. Don't worry about it; just accept it and you'll be a whole lot happier and back in control of your emotions.

Lateral differences

From time to time, you may also get caught up in lateral differences that don't have anything to do with gender. One of these differences is that some of us are the type of people who tell it like it is, or get straight to the point of what we are trying to communicate, while others prefer to suggest or beat around the bush. For example, a person who wants to go to the cinema may say, 'lets do something tonight, maybe the cinema or something' where as someone else may prefer to say, 'I'd like to go to the cinema tonight'. Differences like this are small things that can become irritants very early on in a fledgling relationship if two people are opposite types. In this example, it is well worth establishing, when you first meet someone whether he is a 'say it straight' person or a 'go round the houses' type, and arm yourself effectively if things start to develop between you.

Key values

It is even more important to establish exactly what your root values are in a relationship, and thoroughly understand them so you are able to relay them to him as your relationship develops. Your future partner doesn't necessarily have to have the same values as you, as long as he understands what is important to you and likewise you understand what is important to him. For example, below is a list of the usual values most people would say were important to them. You may put 'feeling respected and important to him' high on your list, however, he may not recognise it is quite so important to you since it isn't something at the top of his list. Read the list and place the values in order of importance to you.

This is not something you would lay on the line to him in the very early stages of your romance, but you will need to make things clear fairly early on if you are looking for a more harmonious union.

- Feeling loved
- Being able to trust
- Being trusted
- That you are able to express yourself without conflict or misunderstanding
- That your partner recognises and appreciates your support for him
- Enjoying intimacy
- Feeling respected and important to him
- Feeling you have emotional and moral support from him

Contact cravings

Arming yourself with as much information about the 'science' of how a man generally goes about life and romance is of course going to help you enormously when it comes to controlling and managing your emotions. However, sometimes we become so engrossed in our man that we end up in an emotional tizz and our logic and understanding of what we should be doing just doesn't filter through to the way we act and react.

I know how it feels when you check your phone ten times an hour, as you are desperate for him to text or call. I also know how it feels when you can't stop yourself sending him a message 'just in case he lost your number'. However, if you want to successfully complete my LCFR programme, and meet a man for keeps, you have to rein in this kind of damaging, negative behaviour.

In the early stages the LCFR programme, my tasks and disciplines will gradually start to change your behaviour for the better without you realising it's happening, but there will come a time, perhaps after the first date with someone you particularly liked, when you'll want to make contact with him. You'll feel drawn to your phone or will be desperate to email and instigate contact – just to see if he's thinking of you. If you feel these 'contact cravings' coming on, here's how to stop yourself wrecking your potential new romance.

1. Set yourself a target day Pick a day, say seven days after your date. Mark it on your calendar and make sure you *do not* contact him before then. With luck, and if he likes you, you should hear from him within the week.

2. Extend If by the seventh day there's still no word, give yourself an extension. Add on another three or four days and stay strong.

3. Man-ipulate If by the time your second target day is reached you still haven't heard from him, then I'll allow you *one text only*. But you have to be clever and make it seem unrelated to your date. If you are a well-skilled 'man-ipulator', (and remember I believe manipulation is a positive virtue), you'll have found out a few things about him on your date like the football team he supports or which sport he follows. Use this information as an excuse to text or email him. For example, 'I notice Arsenal got a battering at the weekend' or 'Poor old Tiger Woods is still not back on his game'. But once you've pressed send you *must* leave it there. This is a one-off luxury and the one and only time I'll allow you to instigate contact. *Do not* add on anything extra such as 'would be nice to see you again' or 'when can we catch up'. And **under no circumstances** do you add a kiss. Remember, you want to make him feel you are worth chasing.

4. The follow up If he texts you back, don't continue the conversation or respond unless his message actually asks for a reply. If he wants to continue the conversation, leave it at least six hours until you reply. Just be happy to have heard from him. His contact should give your self-esteem enough of a boost to wait it out again.

5. No contact? If he doesn't message you back, write him off. Put him out of your mind and out of your heart. Do *not* humiliate yourself by making contact again, especially if all you want to do is send a rude and resentful message. Walk away with your head held high and your pride intact. Believe me, there are lots of other men out there. I meet them day in day out and listen to them telling me they want to get married and have kids!

Now I know what you are thinking – why should we girls have to go through all this? Why can't men just call us the day after the date? You must remember that a man is following his desire to hunt you down. If you take the chase away from him and offer yourself up on a plate, he'll drop you straight away or go along with it for the sake of a quick fling, then be off hunting a more challenging woman. Too many women make the mistake of being pushy and not posing themselves as a challenge, often because they have low self-esteem or they just don't want to risk letting this one get away. It makes it too easy and your date will not bother with you again – plus it isn't a particularly feminine trait.

When a guy decides to settle down with a woman, he wants to feel like he has worked really hard to get her; it makes him feel that she is special. If a woman has no self-belief it is difficult for any man to have belief in her.

TV producer, Charlotte, was a 28-year-old stunning blonde. She came across as the woman who had it all: her own apartment, a great job, natural beauty. Sophisticated and stylish, every man I introduced her to was smitten and couldn't wait to take her on a date. But despite looking and acting the part, no man wanted to take her on a second or third date. Why, I wondered? Then I began to hear the same feedback from every client. Silly Charlotte was so desperate to settle down that she became a 'virtual' stalker of every man she met.

After hearing the same story from four different dates, I decided to take action. I joined her at a singles event and watched as she swatted away every man who came near her. She was so cool; she worked those guys perfectly. Every man in the room was trying to catch her attention. But when they made an approach, she gave them the instant brush off and then she would lean in and tell me 'wow, he was gorgeous'. To me, it seemed she posed herself as a natural challenge. I began to question the feedback I had received from the men she had met.

Then a male friend of mine joined us at the bar. We had a quick drink together and I left the event, leaving them together. Later that evening I got a text from my friend saying 'wow' and thanking me for introducing them. He told me he had worked very hard to win her over and persuade her to give him her number.

But the next week my friend called me and asked, 'is she always like this?' When I asked him to explain, I was staggered by Charlotte's dreadful behaviour. My friend had texted her the next lunchtime, asking if he could take her out the following weekend. But instead of graciously replying 'yes', Charlotte had fired back 'why not tonight?' He explained he had an early plane to catch the next morning and didn't want to

Continued over page...

Continued from previous page...

travel miles to meet her that night. She promptly told him she would drive to his house! Against his better judgement he agreed, as he believed she was 'out of his league' and he wanted to continue his chase.

Charlotte arrived with a bottle of champagne and pounced on him the moment he opened the door. They had wild sex. She then told him, as she'd never had a one-night stand she was staying the night and having breakfast with him! He tried to get her to change her mind, but she had brought an overnight bag and declared she had drunk too much to drive.

The next morning he fled his house to catch his flight, leaving her in bed. Before he reached the airport, Charlotte had bombarded him with 17 texts. More came thick and fast throughout the day.

My friend managed to escape Charlotte's web by falsely claiming he was still hung up on his ex – and was hit by a barrage of horrific abuse from her. A week had passed when he contacted me and she still hadn't let up. Here was a beautiful girl who from the outside was a catch, but who had such low self-esteem she was prepared to throw herself to any man who showed an interest.

I called her and explained this wasn't the right way to go about things, but she lied, pretending my friend had stalked her. I mentioned all her other dates said the same thing and asked her to consider therapy or coaching, but she was in denial and made an excuse for each of the men.

I didn't hear from Charlotte for three years. The next time she made contact with me, she mentioned that she had got pregnant the year before and was now the mother of a beautiful three-month-old baby, but that the father had dumped her while she was still pregnant.

I wonder why?

Of course, Charlotte is an extreme example, but many women – even if we hate to admit it – have a little of Charlotte in us. We start off the right way by letting men come after us, but then forget how well this works. Before we know it, the men are on the run with us chasing them, losing every shred of dignity along the way.

The 'fast forward' woman

Contrary to what most women think, men are *not* commitment phobic, nor are they reluctant to settle down. They simply want to ensure they are settling down with the right girl.

Most men do want to marry and have kids, but they don't want to be rushed. The one type of woman men generally avoid is a 'fast forward' woman. These are the girls that are planning marriage and babies after the third date. They want a declaration of love within weeks, and a ring on their finger in six months, or in some cases even sooner. They will ask at every step of the relationship 'where is this going' just to reassure themselves they are not wasting time.

Guys want time to check you out, to see if you'll make a good wife or mother. Force the issue, and you could lose him. Let commitment come naturally, with him suggesting it to you, and you'll hook him for life.

Most men who join my dating agencies tell me they are scared stiff of becoming a 'baby making machine'. Many men in their late 30s or 40s will steer clear of women the same age for just this reason. They feel dating a woman in this age group won't allow them much time to really get to know her and find out if she is Miss Right. They are terrified they'll be bounced into being a dad – just like the man who fathered Charlotte's child in the case history above – and then be involved in a messy split if she turns out not to be 'the one'.

If you're younger, time is on your side and you have many years to make your choice of partner. When you reach your mid-30s, things aren't quite so straight-forward. You may feel your time to become a mum is running out; your biological clock may be ticking; or you may have set yourself a deadline of getting married and having a baby by the time you hit 40. All these things are possible, but you have to be clever about it. No man wants a woman who seems desperate. A 'fast forward' woman is hard enough for a man to handle, but a 'fast forward' woman with declining child bearing years is seen as too much of a risk, no matter how much sex appeal she has.

Women between the ages of 36 and 47 need to be at the top of their game to make the most of their romance opportunities. You'll be competing for men with women in their late 20s, so this isn't the time to let the weight creep on, to be unfit, to shun stylish outfits for comfy casual wear. This is the time to push your boundaries and be the best you've ever been.

On the plus side, age brings sophistication and experience. You'll hopefully have confidence on your side, be more sensual than a younger woman, more worldly and captivating – all of which helps turn a man's head. Work on offering him the best from every angle, and try to appear extremely laid back about rushing into anything, and you'll have more than enough to overcome the younger competition. However, you may need to date more, meet more men, and work at it harder than a younger girl. Redouble your efforts; look at every new event and activity as an opportunity to meet someone.

CASE STUDY TWO

Catherine was already 40 when I met her. She'd divorced two years previously after her husband cheated on her, and was left devastated when the 'other woman' gave birth to her husband's baby on the day their split was finalised. Desperate for kids herself, she flung herself at any man who gave her a first glance, never mind a second. Men could smell her panic – and hear the deafening tick-tock of her biological clock! Catherine was good at getting first dates, but rather than make light conversation, she'd grill each man about his plans for a family, even asking which month he'd prefer his children to be born! Any man that braved a second date – and there were very few – immediately came under pressure for a 'weekend away' with her. They fled, fearing she was hatching a baby-making plan.

But putting aside her fears about never becoming a mum, Catherine had a lot going for her. She worked as a translator, was educated, attractive and could hold a charming conversation with anyone she met.

Continued...

My job was to convince Catherine she wasn't on the scrapheap, but still held a good hand of cards in the game of life.

Before she began dating again, I insisted she started counselling sessions to come to terms with her divorce. We worked on her fitness and her wardrobe to ensure she looked the best she could. And when she was ready to date, I banned her from mentioning the B word (babies) or the M word (marriage) for the first six months of any relationship. I don't doubt it was torture for her, but to her credit, she stuck to it. She realised how, by holding back on what you want, you can sometimes reach it faster. Men began to see her as a sophisticated, sexy catch not a crazed baby machine. She was no longer a 'fast forward' woman but someone who men had to work hard to win over.

Aged 42, Catherine met a doctor called Oliver. At 47, he was older but had never married as he'd worked so hard building up his practice. Oliver was entranced by her and they married nine months after meeting. Catherine now has her longed-for baby – a girl who was born when Catherine was 44.

Catherine made it in the nick of time to have a baby by stopping piling on the pressure – but had she continued to try to 'fast forward' men, I have no doubt she'd still be single and childless.

The cougar

Many women ask my opinion on dating younger men. I can tell you for sure that single men in their late 20s and early 30s love an older woman. Usually they've grown tired of picking up young girls in clubs and bars every night – but they are not quite ready to settle down. They want a regular girlfriend, but not one who is after marriage and babies just yet.

Instead of 'Miss Right' many men this age go for 'Ms Right Now'. Their perfect scenario is a fit, attractive, older woman in her mid-40s. They prefer her to have had children when she was much younger, or got past the stage where she feels broody. She is usually more confident than women of his own age, she's more worldly, well travelled and self-sufficient with her own regular income. What's more, she will usually be far more sexually aware, which every man – old or young – loves. A younger guy gains so much from this type of liaison, and may prefer it to having a regular girlfriend nearer his own age who hassles him about 'getting serious' before he is ready.

However, the 'cougar', as older women who date younger men are known, should be aware she's only her cub's 'Ms Right Now'. This type of relationship rarely has any real longevity. While some men do genuinely fall in love with their cougar, most see the partnership as a sexy 'safety net' where they have fun, regular sex, exciting dates and no real commitment.

Eventually, as the man gets older, his mind turns to marriage and starting his own family – which an older woman cannot provide. Society's rules and peer pressure usually turn his attentions to someone closer to his own age who can give him the children he craves. If the cougar can handle this eventual outcome, without day dreaming that she'll grow older with her cub, then she can have a whole lot of fun. If you are eligible for 'cougar' status, I can tell you from personal experience, it will probably be one of the most fulfilling, easy going and enjoyable relationships you have ever embarked upon. However, if you find yourself in this situation, while enjoying your younger man, keep your options open for a longer-term lover closer to your own age.

When Serena met Eamon he was 28 and she was 44. She was extremely attractive – slim, fit and active for her age – and had already had two children in her mid-20s. Despite the big age difference, they had fantastic chemistry and made a great couple. After a year together, Eamon moved into Serena's place. Eamon thought he had landed on his feet, swapping a pokey bachelor flat for a sprawling house. But right from the start he kept his options open, renting out his flat rather than selling it. Lovesick Serena, however, thought this union was for life.

Their first year or two of living together was bliss. They holidayed together, partied every weekend and the sex was fantastic. But things began to change as Serena grew older. She was content to stay home and snuggle up on the sofa, but Eamon still wanted to hit top bars, restaurants and nightclubs. Gradually he started to go out more on his own.

The couple spent eight years together, but towards the end Serena took on a 'mother' role, rowing with Eamon about the 'boys' nights out'. Deep down Serena knew he might eventually find someone else. Like many cougars, she was never really secure in the relationship. She dreamed of marriage, but he was happy to just glide along until his 'Ms Right' appeared.

The inevitable happened, and Eamon met someone at work nearer his own age. The romance blossomed and he left Serena at 52, alone with a broken heart. Two years later, she is still not over him. But if she'd kept her options open, and enjoyed the relationship for what it was, perhaps she would be in a different place emotionally right now.

Chapter Four

Understanding the
laws of attraction

Chapter Four Understanding the laws of attraction

Understanding what makes us attracted to another person is one of the biggest challenges in the dating game. In the decade I have been matching couples it has become clear that while many of us dream of the perfect relationship, very few of us understand what it takes to reach this 'holy grail'.

Most women have a fixed idea of their 'Mr Perfect'. Perhaps he's 6ft (1.8m) tall, is a lawyer or a doctor, wears sharp suits, earns a fortune and has a manly physique and chiselled jaw. We convince ourselves we will allow a flaw or too, but we are really looking for someone almost perfect. He is our dream man – but that's all he is – a dream. Unless you are the female equivalent of him, with a supermodel figure, stunning looks, a designer wardrobe and fabulous career, and I'm talking Elle McPherson types here, it's highly unlikely you'll land a man with all the qualities you are ultimately seeking.

However, as I've relayed to you previously in this book, many women I meet are so stuck on meeting this dream man that they ignore most other great Mr Maybe's around them. They plough all their energy into trying to find a man who matches up to the fantasy, and dismiss dozens of lovely guys for trivial reasons like the wrong job or being two inches too short; he already has children or he lives too far away.

Women who come to me looking for love convince themselves they are open minded, but 80 per cent are hung up on this non-existent fantasy. It's only when I convince them to date outside their 'wish list', and they fall in love with someone they'd never have looked at before, that they realise how many years they've wasted chasing an illusion that doesn't exist.

Sometimes I get so frustrated I could climb onto the rooftops and shout: 'Ladies, have the nous to kiss the frog that turns into the prince, rather than pinning your hopes on going straight for the prince!'

What your wish list should contain

Let's take a look at your probable wish list.

My guess is it looks a little like this:

Wish list one: the 'superficial' wish list
1. Tall and attractive
2. Successful and confident
3. Has a sense of humour
4. He earns as much as me or more
5. He is honest and loyal
6. He is attuned to your wishes with regard to children
7. He is generous

If you want to find a man sooner rather than later, you should look at refining your list. Is it realistic? Why not start working towards a 'real love' version – the one that will find you real happiness?

Wish list two: real love
1. He is confident and masculine
2. He has old-fashioned values about wanting to look after me.
   I don't necessarily need him to provide for me but I do want him to look after me and do his utmost to protect me in any way he can. (Not in a heavyweight boxer sort of way, merely that he is supportive, lends you his jacket on a cold night, de-ices your car in the mornings, etc.)
3. He has ambition. (He might be a very successful man, but he might be a guy who is on his way to the top. Sometimes a good woman can be the difference between a regular guy and a successful man.)
4. He is loyal
5. He is honest (Whatever happens, whatever mistakes he makes, you know he will face up to things.)
6. He is attuned to your wishes with regard to children

You'll notice that there are two or three qualities on both wish lists. These are non-negotiable qualities that all *good* men must have. The rest of the points on wish list one are just not important, because none of them will bring you lasting love and happiness. Let us look at some of the reasons why.

Looks

While we may all want a good-looking man, you should be open to dating less attractive men, as even the ugliest guy can be made over into someone far more appealing. Once you are dating him, you can work wonders with his image. I've seen below average men transformed into something very special with a bit of styling work, new shoes and a new hair cut. It doesn't take much time and it's far easier to work on a male makeover than a female one. A man can even still look attractive when carrying a bit too much weight if he has all the other qualities going for him.

Salary

Women can stress far too much about a guy's salary. Once a man feels settled and happy, with your help he can be steered to do better financially. If you are driven, then it's important, though not essential, he has that ambition. It is essential, however, that he has some sort of drive, even if it is not in his career, otherwise no matter how good-looking he is you'll end up carrying him and resenting him.

Sense of humour

A sense of humour is a bonus but should not be something at the top of your wish list. Most people have some kind of sense of humour, and you'll find it comes out quite naturally when a man is happy and relaxed. Beware the man who always tries to appear 'funny', as it may be a way of masking his low self-esteem.

Height

I admit it is relatively important for most women to be with a man who is taller. A man likes to feel he can protect his woman, a girl enjoys the feeling of a larger male partner and the dynamics are generally more comfortable if the woman is slightly smaller. However, this is not always the case. Look at Rod Stewart and Penny Lancaster – you couldn't get a happier looking couple. My point is that the average woman is just 5' 4" (1.6m) tall so it is unnecessary for petite women to insist on a man who's 6' (1.8m) plus? Most of the male population are over 5' 5" (1.7m) so this shouldn't really pose a problem. Women can sometimes be their own worst enemy when it comes to finding and keeping a man. Sticking to a height restriction is one way to ensure you never meet anyone who measures up.

Loyalty

This is an essential quality on every woman's list. A man without loyalty is no man at all. I've known so many women be supportive to their partners and partially responsible for their man's success, only to see them dumped for a lustful thrill. If you find your man has been unfaithful, you may still be able to save the relationship – but only if he is genuinely remorseful and only if it happens once. If he comes crawling back begging forgiveness and realises how pathetic and weak and stupid his actions were, then you may have a chance. However, a serial cheat or a man who refuses to admit wrong-doing is someone you would be best to avoid getting involved with.

A loyal man is one that recognises your role in making him who he is and appreciates you all the more for it. A loyal man won't look outside the relationship, as long as you are doing what you can to make him happy. Recognising and encouraging loyalty in a man early on in a fledgling relationship can save much heartache in later years.

CASE STUDY

Jerry, 43, was an intelligent woman who ran her own consultancy business. She was doing well, making money, travelling frequently and socialising with her clients. But she just couldn't meet a man.

When she came to see me it was obvious why. The negativity oozed out of her. The first thing she said, before she even sat down, was 'I doubt if you can help me' followed swiftly by 'all the best men are either married or gay'.

As we chatted I noticed how tense she was. Jerry was clearly uncomfortable telling me about what she viewed as her 'failure' to have wooed and settled with a man. She had only seen success in her working life and couldn't understand why she didn't have the same success in her love life. In 25 years she had never been in a relationship that had lasted more than a year, and that was only a casual sexual affair. She had no self-belief yet had an air of supremacy and projected the feeling that the world owed her a partner.

Continued...

Visually she had the makings of an attractive woman. She needed to lose weight and gain some sparkle and vibrancy, but this was because she was all work and no play, and could be easily fixed by introducing some outside interests into her life.

When I sent Jerry my brutally honest feedback, she was shocked but agreed to make some changes to improve her chances. The first step was to get her comfortable around men, and I selected some charming guys for her to date. While they may not have been the best-looking men on my books, they were all successful, eligible and fantastic company. And they all wanted to start a family, which Jerry, nearing 44, was still keen on.

But when I sent her their picture and profiles, she rejected every one outright. She sent me a brusque email stating as she was paying me, she expected a far more attractive selection of men. When I quizzed her as to what was wrong with them, her only response was that she didn't fancy any of them.

Now Jerry had made three crucial mistakes: firstly, she'd rejected the men on the strength of a single photo, despite all of them having every single quality she'd requested; secondly, she was asking to date men with looks way out of her league; and thirdly, she wanted all of this before she'd done much to improve herself visually.

When Jerry rejected the first three profiles, I promptly sent her three more. But this time they were profiles of visually extremely attractive men. Jerry immediately agreed she'd be happy to date all three. However, I had to inform her that none of the men found her photo or profile appealing and had all turned her down. Unknown to Jerry, the first three she rejected had also turned her down. Not because they didn't find her attractive, but because they all felt she seemed 'bland'.

Continued over page...

Continued from previous page...

Jerry was an extreme example, but like so many successful, single women today, her expectations far outweighed what she had to offer. She thought that by paying a dating agency she would automatically be presented with a movie star who would fulfil all her dreams.

You have to realise this isn't going to happen. You'll only get out of life what you put in, and if you're not offering much in the dating stakes, no man is going to back you as his life partner. If Jerry hadn't managed it herself in 25 years, I couldn't do it for her in a few weeks.

My job with Jerry was to hone and improve what she could offer, so she could present herself as a better catch to the kind of men she wanted – and to look at those she had previously dismissed.

Being attractive comes from within. Whatever you starting point, you can always improve, and the more you improve, the better your chances are of meeting someone to love.

Chapter Five

Rediscover your femininity
and release your
womanly charms

Chapter Five Rediscover your femininity and release your womanly charms

As I explained earlier, femininity is one of your most powerful tools of attraction. In this chapter I'm going to reveal some very special secrets on how to make the best of yourself and maximise your womanly charms and ultimately your appeal. A feminine woman is a woman with oodles of sex appeal – in a man's eyes this and femininity go hand in hand. So what does a man find feminine?

- A graceful woman
- A woman who doesn't want to control him
- Someone who looks and smells clean
- A woman who takes pride in herself
- The way a woman walks and moves
- A shapely figure
- A good homemaker
- A woman who has self-esteem
- A woman who isn't a man hater
- A woman who has strength of character
- A woman surrounded by a vibrant aura of energy

This list hasn't just been dreamed up; it has been compiled over many years by getting men's feedback on what they found feminine after their successful dates and what they found unfeminine when a date didn't go so well. It is very difficult to completely change yourself if you are a bit of a tomboy, or if you are lacking in womanly charms, but if you are at least aware of what men are seeking you can possibly sharpen up on some of these virtues.

Maximising your appeal

My number one piece of advice for women who have not been dating on a regular basis is to build a 'band of men' around you. A woman who has five or six men vying for her attention is going to be in a much better place mentally than a woman who has no male attention at all. Flirt with these men; have some natural banter going with them to practise your conversation skills, as it will help you learn to relax around the opposite sex. You don't have to pretend to fancy them; just learn to keep them at a distance in a charming and graceful manner. It will be perfect practice and will help you behave naturally when you meet someone who really appeals.

I know many single women who tell themselves they are ready to fall in love, yet very few actually are. In trying to rush things forward you could actually be slowing down the process of finding love, as you'll feel uncomfortable and awkward with any man you find sexy. Practising for a few months during stage one of the LCFR programme shouldn't be viewed as a waste of time. So many women wail that they are too busy to bother dating, and continually date men they don't see as a potential partner, but I know from experience, working on these 'band of men' tactics will undoubtedly have you radiating confidence and sensuality – and ready to attract the right type of man. It is no waste of time at all; it is all about preparing you. It doesn't matter how much you think you are ready, a woman who has not been dating regularly is rarely ready or prepared for falling in love.

Figure it out

The next issue to address is your appearance. You may tell yourself it's what is inside that matters, and to a certain extent that's true, but men are very visual creatures and I can guarantee you'll always have more and better men to pick from as a voluptuous size 12 than a dumpy size 16. Losing weight and improving your figure will also do wonders for your own self-esteem. A woman in good shape can experiment more with her style and dress more fashionably; she'll feel more feminine and be more likely to want to invest in beautiful lingerie and show off her womanly charms.

If you feel uncomfortable with your weight, a great way to drop the pounds and feel fabulous is to join a burlesque dancing class. They are usually women only, so there's no need to worry about who might see you – plus the course can be very empowering and teach you how to embrace your femininity. Exercise in any form, whether it's an aerobics class, running or going to the gym, is great for both the body and the mind. Not only will you soon look better, you'll feel it too. There will be so much more choice of men for you if you are in good shape, I can't labour that point home hard enough.

If you're overweight, please don't feel that I'm being prejudicial. I'm not. I'm simply telling you what you need to do to make the most of your chances. On the most basic level a man doesn't want a woman who is bigger than him. A man wants a woman he can feel protective towards, but if you look like a burly rugby player, and you are larger than him, you simply won't inspire those feelings in him. This is something I hear regularly from all men on my books – so it's straight from their mouths. The shape of a woman is a sexual turn on too. A man wants a woman he can 'throw about' in the bedroom to show off his prowess, but if you weigh far more than him he can't do this and he simply won't fancy you. Don't get me wrong, most men will be turned on by a woman with curves. What he doesn't want is someone a stone overweight who describes herself as curvy!

Dress to impress

Whatever your body shape and size, you can always dress it to look better. We all have friends who may be on the larger side but have such great style they can hide any faults and accentuate the best parts of their bodies. Learn to love fashion and dress in the way that suits your shape. Men adore simple outfits like shift dresses, pencil skirts and feminine blouses. They can't stand baggy leisurewear, shapeless smock tops or high-waisted trousers with tummies bulging out. Avoid the fashion statement items such as harem pants or long maxi shapeless dresses; they are a big turn off for men. Jeans are fine, but they need to be a good shape and dress them up with slinky kitten heels or an attractive top. Always apply a little make-up; lip gloss, blusher and mascara are enough for the daytime, and if your nails are not manicured at least have them looking trimmed and clean. Make an effort to hair remove regularly – everywhere! Surveys have shown that one of the worst sexual turn-offs for a man is when a woman hasn't waxed or trimmed 'down there'. Make the effort every time you step outside the front door even, as I so famously said once, if it's just to put the garbage out. You never know who you may meet that day. Men really do appreciate you making the effort. It makes you far more appealing on all fronts.

Wing woman

I know these changes I'm asking you to make are tough. So it's at this stage I advise you to get the help of a 'wing woman' – a trusted pal who will help steer you through so you can get to your goal more rapidly. Choose someone you admire who already has what you want, or a friend who's looking to make the same changes. Don't ask someone you think may sabotage your efforts, as she secretly wants you to stay single. You'll need someone who is honest and can keep you on track as you transform your life. If you can afford it, you can pay a life coach, but they can be expensive. Your 'wing woman' should be somone you can rely on for honest feedback on how you are progressing at each stage of the LCFR programme – and for a kick up the behind if you're not! (Wing woman services are available at www.coffeeandcompany.com)

What appeals to a man?

So now you know how to make the very best of yourself, let us look at what men *really* want. These are the seven points almost every man I've ever met has asked for in a potential partner, and every one of my seven points is simple and achievable. They are all within your grasp.

1. That she's attractive: All a man is asking for here is that you've made a little bit of an effort. Look clean and smell fragrant, even if you're working the natural look. Have a good haircut, clean nails and sparkling teeth. Shave or wax your legs and armpits and anywhere else that needs it! If you have the cash, get your eyebrows professionally shaped, as it will make a huge difference to your face. Use moisturiser and body cream. Take care of yourself from top to toe.
2. That she doesn't emasculate him: Don't be pushy or bossy or try to wrestle control all the time. Listen to what he has to say. If you need to take the lead, do it in a subtle manner that still leaves him feeling like the man of the relationship.
3. Respect: Let your man take praise without pushing yourself as his saviour or mentor. Relish the fact that others look up to him, rather than trying to hog his limelight.
4. That she has 'backbone': A man wants you to come across as strong, calm and ready for what life may throw at you as a couple. He doesn't want someone who plays the victim or is hysterical. While every woman has weak moments, don't allow yourself to wallow in self-pity. Just pick yourself up and get on with it and he'll love you all the more.
5. That she's positive: A woman with upbeat, vibrant energy will always have men in love with her. You can have fabulous looks and a stunning figure, but if you radiate anger or misery men will avoid meeting you again.
6. Self-respect: Respect yourself and everyone else will too.
7. She's special: Clever women make their man feel he's incredibly lucky to be with her. You should never tell him this, but make him realise it every day by being all the things he wants. Also, try and have a little uniqueness about you. It's no good just being smart – there are loads of smart women – know something about something that is rare.

Chapter Six

Avoiding the relationship
agenda trap

Chapter Six Avoiding the relationship agenda trap

The two questions I get asked the most by women are: 'Why didn't he call?' and 'Why won't he commit?' There is a very simple answer, but it needs a lot of explaining. I'm warning you now that you may feel like hurling this book across the room at certain points during this chapter, but stick with me. Everything I'm explaining has been gleaned from listening to men and women and seeing how things pan out – it's all very true, very good advice, even if you don't like the sound of it. Follow what I'm advising to the letter, even if you don't like it, and you won't be single for much longer.

A lot of what goes on in a man's mind is instinctive. They don't think about the way they behave – the just do it. Much like a tantrum-throwing two-year-old or a surly teenager, their behaviour may seem strange or even anti-social, but its part of who they are.

So why is it that we can accept the way a naughty toddler or grumpy teenager acts, but we can't let a man be a man? When tots misbehave or teens stop communicating, we write it off to age or hormones. But instead of letting men be men, we get upset and aggressive at their behaviour. Modern women become incredulous that a man wants to call the shots, and furious that they can't control him or where the relationship is going.

Why didn't he call?

Let's talk about a very common example. Why do we have to wait for the man to call us? Of course it seems unfair and many women think it's ridiculous that in the 21st century we can't pick up the phone and tell a guy what we feel. Women get so upset when I recommend waiting to let their date call them. Often they listen to their friends who whisper, 'Yes, text him, call him, what harm can it do? At least you'll know then whether you were in his thoughts and maybe move things along at the pace you want things to go.' Then they go against my advice and call or text – and then rarely hear from him again.

Of course, it's up to you and you can 'take control' and make contact first after a date. However, by doing that you run the risk of turning him off not on. I'm telling you in no uncertain terms that even the most subtle, post-first-date text will smother any passion he has for you – and it's all because of male biology. A man is driven by testosterone to hunt and chase, and if you make it too easy then he'll lose interest.

Now I'm not saying any of this is fair – and it's certainly not very 21st century – but it's just the way it is. You can choose to fight it and be single, or accept it and fall in love. The decision is yours. So we already know if you text a guy after the first date before he's made contact, he's unlikely to call you. But there can also be other reasons why he doesn't ring. Let's look at why.

If he doesn't call immediately it could be because he doesn't fancy you. This can cover a whole host of reasons, including:

- He didn't find you visually appealing
- He didn't find you captivating or vibrant enough
- He didn't enjoy the way you made him feel; perhaps you emasculated him slightly
- You didn't appear to believe in yourself, so he found it hard to see you as a prize worth chasing
- You didn't allow him to use his adrenalin-driven instincts to woo you (in other words you posed yourself as no kind of challenge)

Although we like to make up 'good' excuses as to why he didn't call, the reason he didn't call is *unlikely* to be:

- Because he found you intimidating
- He got into an accident on the way home
- He is gay

Or it may be he *does* fancy you, but doesn't call immediately. This, as I've said before, could be because:

- He doesn't multi task as well as most of us women do and has a lot on in his life so chooses to put off the chase for a while
- He prefers to wait until he feels at his best before beginning the chase
- He is in another relationship and has decided to stay loyal to her
- He is casually seeing someone else and would prefer to end it before beginning something with you

Men are made to chase, hunt and fight for something worth having. If you're the type of woman that snatches that power from him, you'll also dash your chances of a great relationship with him. Please don't make this mistake. If you do – and you keep on doing it – you'll stay single for a very long time to come.

Why won't he commit?

For love to grow and last, men need to manage the agenda at every stage of a relationship. A man needs to feel he is calling the shots. In his eyes it's the only way forward, as he needs to feel he's the driving force behind the partnership. No man wants to feel that he is being forced to commit by a scheming woman. It goes back to the masculinity thing – while you may see it that you are planning for the next stage, he may feel pushed, bullied and bounced into something he's not ready for.

I've seen scores of women kill off good relationships by pushing their men too far too fast and falling into what I call the 'agenda trap'. Often the man was on the verge of suggesting a deeper commitment himself, but just like the first date text, if you take his power away from him he'll lose interest. The reason behind it is exactly the same – your man needs to feel he's chasing you and trying to pin you down as his partner. If you make it too easy by suggesting moving in, marriage or a baby, you run the risk of him getting bored.

In a good relationship, you should feel relaxed enough to trust that each stage will happen as it should. There should be a natural flow and rhythm to your partnership. If you feel the need to constantly quiz your partner on what's coming next, take this as a warning sign to back off. You need to step back and shut up – or risk losing him. Use your womanly wiles; man-ipulate and keep cool and you will have your man begging for what you want.

Below I've listed the relationship killer questions you must *never* ask. Let him be the one to suggest each and every stage.

- When are we going to see each other again?
- Where is this relationship heading?
- When can I meet your friends?
- When are you going to invite me to stay at your apartment?
- When can I meet your parents?
- When can we go away for the weekend together?

- When can we go on holiday together?
- When can we move in together?
- When are we going to get married?
- When are we going to try for a baby?

I understand how frustrating this is for you. I know you can manage every other aspect of your life and set your own timetable when it comes to work, social things, friends or family, so it is annoying that, in order to be a success, this is one area of your life where you need to leave it to him to prompt the relationship progression. There's good reason the word is man-age and not woman-age!

If you accept this, go along with it and don't feel resentful that your man is controlling part of your life you'd prefer to be planning, you will find your relationship lasts longer. However, if you can't accept it and continue to force his hand at every key stage, you will continue to be 'unlucky' in love. It doesn't matter how beautiful or charismatic you are. You can be a stunning success in every other aspect of your life, career or challenges and achievements, but if you fall into the dreaded agenda trap you will never be able to hold on to a man.

The only exceptions to this are those women who choose men with no self-esteem. This type of guy is happy to be bullied, browbeaten and told what to do – but do you want to spend the rest of your life with someone like that? There are a few poor excuses for men who are on the lookout for a mother figure, who'll take charge of every aspect of his existence, but unless you are happy to give up everything else you dreamed about in a relationship, avoid at all costs.

If a relationship isn't moving at the pace you would like, don't try issuing ultimatums. This is pointless and weakens your position. You can't force a man into a decision through threats; it's unfeminine, looks desperate and is highly unlikely to work. Look at it from his point of view. If he says yes to your plan, it's only to keep the peace and he'll end up resenting you; if he says no, you've lost him and wrecked your relationship.

So let's reflect — to avoid the agenda trap, you must:

- Always wait for your date to call you after you have met
- Always wait for the guy to progress the relationship at his pace
- Never give ultimatums if the relationship is not moving at your preferred pace

The fledgling relationship

Let's get one thing straight. Just because you've had two dates with a new man, it doesn't mean he's your boyfriend. Many women try to fast forward here and rush the man into a committed partnership before he is ready.

Try and train yourself to thinking that the first few months of any relationship make it a 'fledgling relationship'. You are testing each other out, laying the groundwork and putting down boundaries for the partnership to work. It may feel very intense and you may be madly in love, but it's still early days.

If the romance goes past four dates, it's clear he has a genuine interest in you. In a man's eyes, you are passing his basic tests. However, before you officially become his 'girlfriend' or 'partner' you have to pass through the 'irritating stage'. He wants to know if he can put up with everything:

- The hours you keep
- Your dress sense
- Are you too loud or too quiet?
- Your attitude to money – spendthrift or miser?
- Do you like the same food or music as he does?
- Can he handle your habits, your leanings?

The list goes on, and what's on it is very personal to each guy. But in fairness to your new man, you may be asking the same questions about him. Every man will have his own rules on what he will and won't put up with, and the older men get the less flexible they are with it. Older men can become set in their ways, making it tougher for a woman to pass this stage of the fledgling relationship.

If you're falling into the 'fast forward' trap, and trying to push him through this stage too soon, you'll annoy the hell out of him and he'll give up. Instead, view it as time to get to know each other's quirks and habits – a time for you to make sure he's someone that will suit you.

The fledgling stage of the relationship could go on for months, but if it gets to six months and he's evasive about normal relationship milestones (see chart over page), be watchful that he's totally honest and open with you. Do this discreetly; there are few things men dislike more than being monitored.

Normally if a man has been dating you, even on a casual basis, for three or four months and all seems well, he should start to introduce you to some of his friends and refer to you as his girlfriend. Four to six months is also a healthy stage of relationship development to be thinking about or embarking on a holiday or break together – then you can move on to a more permanent relationship. Take a look at my relationship development milestone chart below, so you can measure your progress.

Milestone	Relationship development	Time scale
Initial interaction	Flirting/register initial interest in each other	Immediately
First date request	He's trying to find out if you're keen on him	Within a few hours (the *one time* a girl can press ahead and instigate)
First date	The first big test: do you get on?	Within a couple of weeks of date request
The follow-up	If he's keen, he'll get in touch within a couple of weeks	This could take up to six weeks – stay cool
Second date	He likes what he sees	More likely to be sooner if he likes what he sees – within two weeks
Third date	A chance to get to know you more deeply	Within two weeks of the second date
First month: how many times does he need to be calling you?	He's starting to view you as a potential partner	He calls you 2 or 3 times a week, or more
Sleep together	A big deal: are you sexually compatible	After the fifth or sixth date at least

Milestone	Relationship development	Time scale
How many times a week does he need to be seeing you?	This could depend on location, etc	Between once and five times a week after the first month
Meeting his friends	A big deal: will they rate you? Men want their friends to feel they have done well	During first month
Meeting your friends	Watch his interaction. Is he friendly, not flirty?	During the first or second month
Girlfriend/ boyfriend	The first real time he sees you potentially as for 'keeps'	Month two or three
Weekend away	A whole 48 hours together	Three or four months into your relationship
The 'L' word	This is different for everyone; don't rush it. It's better to say it once he has declared his love for you.	Three months to 12 months
Leaving items at each other's homes	Proof you're comfortable together and staking your claim on each other	Six months into your relationship
Meeting the parents	A major milestone. He is asking his parents to vet you as a potential long-term partner	Six to 12 months into the relationship
Holiday	A sign you are a real couple, as you're putting time and money into being with each other	Six to 12 months into the relationship
Moving on, moving in?	The next step	Eight months to three years into relationship

These time scales should give you a good idea if the relationship is progressing at a healthy level. Obviously location has a lot to do with things. If you live miles away from each other, things may take a little longer in the early stages but could quicken up later. Remember, if things are not progressing at the rate you would like, 'man-ipulate' rather than push.

Moving on and getting what you want

So if you can't call him and can't ask what's next in the relationship, what **can** you do? Plenty. The very best way is to play a clever game and, as just mentioned, 'man-ipulate' him at every stage.

I'm going to ask you to do something that may feel wrong, but it works wonderfully. Even if you are head over heels with your man, you need to keep your options open. Make sure you:

- Still meet other men, if only for a coffee (never become intimate with other men while in a relationship, even a fledgling relationship, or you risk losing your man's trust)
- Keep your online dating profiles open and active, if less flirtatious
- Flirt tamely with other guys on nights out
- Drop hints casually to him if other men have paid attention to you while you've been away from him

If you stop doing any of these you make everything too easy for him. But if you carry on posing yourself as a challenge, then he knows he has to fight hard to win you. You don't need to say a word, but if he knows other men are interested in you, he'll bring forward every landmark point in the relationship to keep you.

I'm **not** suggesting you cheat on your man or become intimate in any way with another man in the hope you might jolt some sense into him, but you should keep your options open until he fully commits. You're doing nothing wrong. Six months into the relationship, it's far better for him to start quizzing you as to why you are still seeing other men, than for you to be asking 'where is this relationship heading?' Once he does ask why you are seeing other guys, you've got him hooked. You can answer the question quite innocently by saying, "Darling I had no idea we were at the point in our relationship that you wanted to be exclusive. You've never made that clear." Then you can add, "Of course, if you want me to stop seeing other men and take the relationship to another level I'm open to discuss that." This is his cue to take things to the next level – perhaps by suggesting moving in together or getting engaged.

It's all the art of 'man-ipulation'. It's the feminine thing to do and he will love you for it. He feels he is in control and believes the ball is still in his court – but you've engineered the situation where you get what you want. It's win–win for you both. Once he's staked his claim on you exclusively, he's unlikely to back down and let you keep your options open; and rather than wriggling out of the crunch 'where's this going?' question, he'll feel he is the one driving the relationship forward.

Of course, you run the risk that he may not care when he finds out you're still seeing other men. In this case, you need to ask yourself if he is the one you want to be with for the rest of your life? Men are very territorial, and if he really isn't bothered the signs don't look good. Use the options you've been keeping open to find yourself someone else. Flirt harder with other men, go on more online dates and find someone better to move on to.

It may also be that he's just lazy. Plenty of men stay in a relationship simply because it is comfortable, even though they are still hoping someone better will come along. Don't let yourself get into this situation. You deserve better than a man that barely cares about you.

By following my LCFR programme, you'll have more choice of men than at any other time in your life. Make sure you use all of the options available to you. As the saying goes, never put your eggs in one basket. I wouldn't advocate exclusively dating one man until he's given you a rock-solid commitment – like that longed for engagement ring!

Chapter Seven

How to maintain
a harmonious romance

Chapter Seven How to maintain a harmonious romance

You've met a man and you're both keen to take it further. You like him and he seems to like you – so what can go wrong? Plenty! If maintaining a relationship was simple, no one would ever get divorced and there would be no need for the multi-million pound relationship counselling industry. The sad fact is statistics show 75 to 80 per cent of all relationships fail. Even marriages where both parties should be fully committed, have a split rate of around two in five.

There are some very simple ways to 'break-up proof' your fledgling relationship and ensure you turn it into a lasting love. The key point to understand is men view relationships very differently to women. While men enjoy the moment women can't rest and constantly have their eye on the next move. Take a simple walk in the park. He's happy in the moment, holding your hand and enjoying your company, but I bet you're tense, worrying if he's going to tell you he loves you or ask if you want to go on holiday with him or move in to his apartment. Women worry so much about what's coming next that if it doesn't happen they are left devastated. You have to remember that there's no reason why it should happen – the man never mentioned whatever it is you are fretting about; it only existed inside your mind.

One happily married man I know likens relationships to asking for directions. A man will gladly bumble around with no idea where he is going but be happy he'll get where he needs to be. A woman, however, wants to plan the route and set off to her timetable and becomes furious if anyone deviates from what she wants. As we've already discovered, no man wants a 'fast forward' woman who tries to push him into commitment before he's ready. So what are the qualities men are looking for when they select a woman to settle down with?

Here's my guide to the vital dos and don'ts, compiled with the help of hundreds of married men:

Don't

- Try to change yourself to be what you think he wants. He fell in love with you as you are – the way you dress, your physical appearance, your interests and sense of humour. Many women change when they meet a man to try to please him further, but he doesn't want you to do that.

- Try to change him. A little tidying up like a new haircut or dress sense over-haul is fine, but don't try to change his interests or his friends. He'll resent you and end it.

- Worry about the small things he does 'wrong'. If he forgets to call you one night, it's not the end of the world – and it isn't the end of the relationship either. He just forgot. Don't blow it up into a big issue and move on.

- Be a doormat. Men don't respect a woman who meekly accepts every instance of bad behaviour. If he **constantly** forgets to call you or **always** lets you down by cancelling dates to meet his mates, he'll just keep taking advantage.

- Stalk him. Calling and texting 40 times a day are not acceptable. Neither is posting intimate messages on social networking sites for the entire world to see. Men don't need constant contact like women.

- Push what's coming next. Be confident the relationship is progressing the right way and at the right pace. Forcing the issue won't make it happen faster; it will only leave you single and back at square one.

- Go to bed without making-up if you have had an argument, and never sulk or nag him. If he doesn't want to do something or tell you where he's been, then no amount of asking is going to get it out of him. Relax, back off and you'll find you won't need to nag at all.

- Over-think and over-analyse. Take a tip from men and accept each moment in the relationship for what it is – and nothing more.

Do

- Make time for him, no matter how busy you are. Although this is easy to do in the first few months, in longer-term relationships, quality time together can easily get forgotten.

- Focus on his good points, not his bad. Remember all men, like all women, will have some faults. But concentrate on what made you fall in love with him in the first place.

- Have sex! Men need more sex than women, but they also use it as proof you love them and find them physically attractive. If you go off sex, a man will think you've gone off him and will be tempted to look elsewhere for a woman who will show him she appreciates him.

- Look after him. There's no need to be a doormat, but occasionally pamper him by cooking him a delicious dinner, running him a bath or giving him a massage. You'd want him to do the same for you, so show how much you appreciate him.

- Lay down boundaries. Men, like little boys, need to know where they stand. It could be something as simple as insisting he does half the housework or doesn't leave wet towels on the bed, but a man with rules to follow is a happy fellow. Men need rules, whether they are playing football, fishing or buying rounds in the pub with their mates.

- Take care of yourself emotionally and physically. Stay attractive to him and try to be positive about your life together, even when you are going through a bad patch. Be that woman he fell in love with.

- Still date. Have fun together, visit places you went when you were falling in love, and make time for a night out at least once a week to keep the special magic alive.

- Praise him and make him feel wanted. Even if it's only asking him to reach for something from a high shelf or put out the heavy bins, men need to feel wanted and masculine. By asking him to help you, you're showing how much you need him.

- Let him treat you if he suggests it, even if money is tight. A man likes to prove he can provide.

- Let him be himself. He may have some hobbies or tastes that you don't like, such as football or heavy metal music, but this is part of who he is. Don't attack or try to change them or he'll see it as an attack on himself.

- Allow the 'boys' night out'. Nothing splits up a new partnership faster than the woman who bans her man from seeing his friends. His mates will jeer he's 'under the thumb', and he'll be staying out to 6am every night to prove them wrong. If you let him have his nights out, it means you can have yours too, if you want.

- Get on with his family. You don't have to like them, but coming up against a man's family – especially his mother – is never a good idea. He has decades of shared history with them, more than he has had with you, so it's unlikely you'll come off better. Cultivate a great relationship with them and they'll become your biggest allies.

- Give him space. Let him go to football, away on a boys' holiday or work late without moaning about it. He'll wonder why you're happy for him to have so much freedom, and gradually you'll find he wants less space. Any woman confident enough to let her man have his own space will have him thinking she has a better offer elsewhere, so he'll stick ever closer to your side.

- Use the 'So what?' test. If you have a row or disagreement, think about whether it really matters or if you're trying to win for argument's sake. Life is too short. Don't waste it on things that don't matter; don't sweat over the small stuff. You can often end up arguing about who said what in the argument more fiercely than the argument you started out with.

- Have a life outside the relationship. Still see your friends and family, go for drinks with your colleagues after work and keep up all your outside interests. Not only will it help keep you a more interesting person, you'll have a support network in place should the relationship fail.

- Believe in yourself. You're a catch so act like one.

- Tell him you love him – every day, even if you have had an argument.

Chapter Eight

The power of positive thinking

Chapter Eight The power of positive thinking

How many women do you know who are 'lucky in love' and always seem to meet the right men? They have a spring in their step, a smile on their face and a great guy by their side while the rest of us look on enviously. You may think they've just got lucky, but there's no so such thing. Lucky people work hard to make their own luck, and they do it through the power of positive thinking.

Psychologists and hypnotherapists have proved if we continually repeat a thought, we can condition our brains to believe it. The brain quite literally builds new neural connections according to what we are telling it to think. So if you're the sort of person who's always moaning 'there are no good men – they are all married, weirdos or gay', then that's what you'll end up believing, and is most probably what will present itself to you. However, if you wake up each day and say, 'today looks great; this could be the day I meet a very special man', then you'll be far happier and in a much better mindset for meeting men. Your brain will be wired and alive to every possibility.

It doesn't stop there either. I firmly believe the way you think effects what you attract in your life. If you think negatively things will go wrong: you'll get ill, friends won't call as they won't want to be around you, and men will steer clear of your miserable little world. But, if you think positively you'll attract the positive: mates will call and ask you on nights out as you're a fun person to be around; you'll get better opportunities at work; you'll look better, feel better, and guys will notice you more. You'll have your own rays of sunshine beaming out from around you.

Positive thinking has helped me through some of the toughest times in my life. I've pulled myself through the most horrendous heartache by focusing my mind on the positive aspects of my life when all around me seemed to be crumbling. It's amazing how you can lift yourself out of a deep depression by being grateful for what you have – and looking forward to what you want. Even at my very worst, I would only allow myself to wallow in upset for a single day and always vowed after a night's sleep to move onwards and upwards.

Positive thinking can help with even the smallest jobs too. I'm writing this at 6am on a Sunday morning, when it would have been all too easy to stay curled up in bed with my partner. Instead, I thought positively, got on with the job, and feel amazing for it. If I'd stayed in bed and put off the writing, I'd have felt lousy for the rest of the day.

You may have read books like *The Secret* by Ronda Byrne and Carolyn Boyes book *Cosmic Ordering in 7 Easy Steps*. If you have read these, you will already know how it's no secret that those people who look on the bright side of life do better in this world. By thinking – and being – positive you are opening yourself up to others around you and the myriad amazing possibilities in this world. Think for a minute about your circle of friends. Isn't it clear that the positive ones cope with whatever life throws at them, and always come up smelling of roses? They have luck on their side because they've gone out of their way to *make* their own luck.

I am so sold on the idea of the power of positive thinking that I use it every day to create even more luck and great things in my life. I don't waste time asking the universe to help me win the lottery; instead, I allow my mind to drift to where I want to be. I keep repeating my hopes, dreams and aspirations and I almost live the feeling in my mind. I imagine I am in my mind's best-case scenario; I imagine how I will feel and I *will* it to happen – and you know what, almost every time it does, and if it doesn't it usually turns out there was good reason why.

So how does this fit in with you meeting a man? Quite simply, you can use it to draw even more romance opportunities your way. Ask yourself honestly, are you always focusing on the worst-case scenario or do you tell yourself everything will come right in the end? If you keep believing and telling your friends that all men are bastards, then I have no doubt it will manifest that way to you. However, change course and keep a picture in your mind of what you want and a strange thing will happen: slowly you'll go from 'wishing' you could find your potential Mr Right to 'knowing' you are going to get him. You'll begin to feel the power of positive thinking. On the rare occasions you don't get all you want, it simply means that path wasn't right for you, but keeping positive will lead you down another equally bright and happy route.

Here is a very effective positive thinking visualisation exercise for you to practise. Keep repeating visualisations while following my LCFR programme, as together they are some of the most powerful tools to find you lasting love.

1. Decide on a good time of day when you can routinely start practising your positive thinking visualisation. If you are a night owl, do it before you drift off to sleep, as you'll awake more rested. Early birds should try it first thing, either sitting with a warm drink or as you stretch and exercise. You can even do it as part of your daily commute, sitting on a crowded bus or train.

Whatever time you decide on, you'll find it pushes all your worries away and your little rain clouds magically evaporate.

2. Don't be embarrassed. Nobody will know what you are doing, so you don't have to be in a quiet place. Simply shut your mind off and begin to think about all the things you would like to happen, just like daydreaming.

3. I find the most effective way is to run through a ritual of 'thanks and please'. Begin by saying thank you in your mind for the health, safety and happiness of your family and friends, and if you are dating, for your partner. Then think about any negative aspects of your life right now, perhaps you're having problems with your boss or you've had a row with your mum, then move on to ask for a resolution. This is also the point to ask for a partner if you are single. You don't have to beg; just ask in a quiet way that's right for you that a good man comes into your life soon. It doesn't have to take long; a few minutes is fine.

4. The idea behind a positive thinking visualisation is to lift away the negative thoughts seeping through your head. When you're weighed down with problems and day-to-day niggles, it's hard to see what you do have going for you. Positive visualisation will temporarily dissolve the problems and allow you to see what you want in your life. Sometimes you can come up with a solution there and then, but often answers pop into your mind later in the day.

5. Make sure you have your regular 'wishes' to go through. Say in your mind how you want things to be, and show gratitude for the way the good things have turned out. For example:

'Thank you for the health, safety and happiness of my friends and family and myself.'

Then move on to your additional dreams and wishes. For example:

'Thank you for helping me to change my approach and for finding me a wonderful man. Thank you for bringing me my soul mate when the time is right for me. Thank you too for bringing me babies.'

Whatever it is you want, ask for it and believe it is going to happen. You can ask for anything you like, but you must believe you are going to get it. You will find your visualisation sessions change your outlook and that you gradually feel sunnier in your everyday life. If you keep it up regularly – and daily is best – I guarantee that positive things will start happening to you.

The power of positive thinking will also ensure you can overcome daily irritations like rude people, road rage and all the nasty parts of modern life you have to put up with. If a car cuts in front of you, resist the temptation to shout, swear and beep your horn. Instead ask yourself is it's really worth it? If you won't remember it in a few weeks time, then who cares? Give out warmth and you will receive it back, and you'll feel much better for not being overcome with anger.

Try positive thinking for a month, even if you're not sure it will work for you. I'm convinced it will make a difference and you will soon see for yourself how you're flooded with optimism – and more men start to ask you out. So get going and start planning what you're going to ask for. Like I have said before, you have nothing to lose and everything to gain.

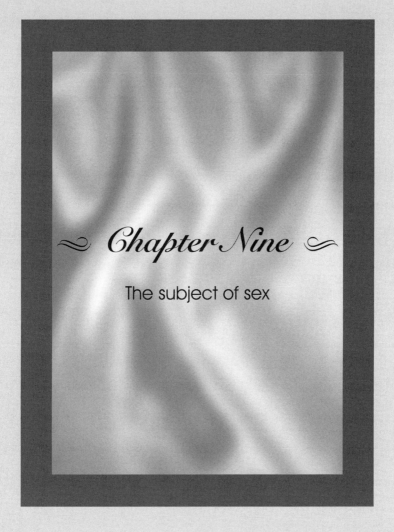

Chapter Nine

The subject of sex

Chapter Nine The subject of sex

I couldn't really complete this book without saying a few words about sex. After all it plays a big part in relationships and the courting process. The most obvious and frequently asked question I receive about sex is 'when should a girl sleep with a guy she is dating?'

There are no hard and fast rules here, but as a guide I think you should have met with him at least four or five times before even contemplating sex. By all means enjoy the kissing and cuddling, but try and leave it just there. A good tip is to avoid alcohol on your initial meetings. Many women have the mindset that there is no point is stopping yourself if you both have a passion for each other. However, it could really go against you if you agree to get intimate too soon.

The point I have laboured all through this book is that every woman **must** pose herself as a challenge in order to create the desire in a man to pursue her, and although you may feel you can't wait to fast forward your liaison to relationship status, you can really mess things up for yourself during the 'fast forward' process. You could establish longevity in the relationship by holding out, and all the time your suitor will become more attached to you mentally and emotionally. If you feel you are a catch, then surely this has got to be the best way to go. OK, so you think you are a wild cat in the bedroom, and perhaps think that if you race ahead to the steamy stuff your date is going to believe his Christmas and birthday have come all at once and he will never let you go, but this really isn't the case. Men simply don't think like that.

What a man wants

Guys, it seems, prefer to savour the intimacy and prolong the actual full-blown sex because they see it all as part of the chase. A recent survey backs this up. An overwhelming 92% of men said they preferred a girl to stall the sex initially when it's a girl they are interested in potentially hooking up with for a more serious romance. Interestingly, when asked how soon they would like to sleep with a girl they were only interested in casually, most men said within two days. So, if you really want to embark on a relationship with your new date, hold off with the sex. And, contrary to what you might want to think, if a guy is pushing for sex soon after meeting you, it's probably because he is only interested in you for precisely just that.

The other thing you should make note of is that when you do eventually get it together on the sexual front, what he does initially isn't likely to be the way he will make love to you on a regular basis. Usually he will try and do everything to impress you. For example, he will probably go down on you the first few times and then gradually this will stop. Don't take offence if this happens. Research has shown us that 71% of men, given the choice, would prefer not to have to do this.

In relation to what a guy likes to happen on the sexual side to your relationship, I have compiled a little list for you below. Assembled together by picking up on what men tell me during their evaluations, and surveys compiled over the last few years, it offers a great insight as to what will win him over between the sheets.

- He likes spontaneity.

- Men prefer to have sex or a sexual encounter almost every time they meet their girlfriend in the early relationship

- Men are just as happy when you perform oral sex on them as they are having full-blown sex

- 88% of men said they get aroused watching porn on the TV

- 76% of those who liked to watch porn said they prefer to do it with their partner than alone

- 31% of men said they liked to experiment and try some things that might be viewed as shocking with their partners sometimes

- 71% of men said they didn't particularly enjoy giving their partners oral sex

- 17% of men said they did not view a fling or one-night stand as being unfaithful

- 13% of men said if they were in love they would forgive their partner if they discovered they had been unfaithful

- 79% of men said they would consider ending the relationship if they didn't find the sex stimulating or if they were not getting enough of it

- Most men have admitted fantasising over other women
  when they are in a relationship

- 83% of men said they thought it weird if a woman didn't
  want to perform oral sex on them

- Overwhelmingly, most men said they preferred their girlfriends
  to wax or at the very least trim down below.

Infidelity

When the topic of sex comes up in discussion, I regularly get asked for my view on infidelity. Most dating dilemma experts will scream 'leave him' if he cheats, however, I think sometimes a moment's lust shouldn't have to crush a relationship to the point of ending it, especially if there are so many positive aspects to the union.

One thing I have learned is that 'perfection' is practically non-existent when it comes to enjoying a harmonious relationship. Whereas I feel a man who constantly cheats and causes heartache would be difficult to live with, I also think that the occasional stupid mistake can be forgiven. As I have mentioned before, if you are not posing yourself as a challenge it would be difficult for any man to sustain his enthusiasm at having you for a partner. Men need the constant stimulation mentally and physically; they need to feel they are constantly punching above their weight. If you don't pose any kind of a challenge and if you are not always slightly keeping him guessing, then this could be enough ammunition to cause him to seek the thrill elsewhere. OK, most men will just absorb themselves into their work or sport or something else to be able to recover the feeling of the hunt, but others will want to go that step further. While we are busy assuming that everything at home is well, he may be tearing his hair out.

With this in mind, it is really important, when you have established some sort of relationship, that sex should be high on the agenda. Men really can't do without it. You also have to remember that if it gets stale and boring you may as well not have any, because boring sex to a man is the same as no sex. It really is down to you to instigate sex and initiate change, because most men won't. They may drop unhelpful hints, but rarely will they actively prompt you to try something new; they will want and expect that to come from you. Again it's all part of keeping yourself posed as a challenge; keeping him guessing so he never knows what you are going to suggest or do.

So in short, I wouldn't always tell you to leave a cheating partner; you have to weigh up in your mind what other aspects there are to his personality that keep you happy. The 50/50 test is always the best. If he is keeping you happy more than 50 per cent of the time, you should stick with him.

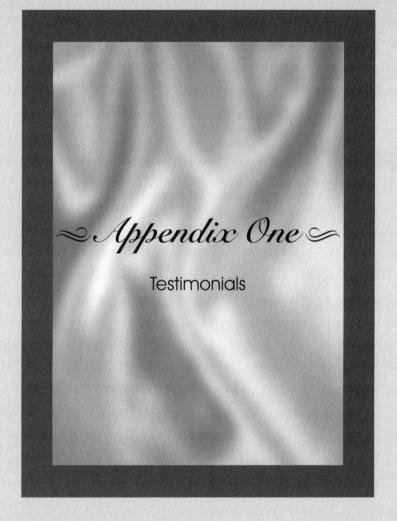

~Appendix One~

Testimonials

Appendix One Testimonials

I have put together some emails and letters I have received from clients over the years, to give you an idea of the ways my CalcuDating System and LCFR programme can assist you in achieving your dream of a happy relationship.

'I felt a bit overwhelmed by the number of guys who seemed to pop up from nowhere after starting your plan; when it rains, it rains a lot of men! I sometimes think you have a challenging job, being in the middle of two sexes and keeping a neutral position. I think you are as genuine, honest and helpful as possible given all that. Your tips do actually work!'

Lydia, 31-year-old doctor from Herefordshire

'Yes I would love to meet him, I trust your judgment completely Lorraine, so far you have me completely sussed.'

Maria, 39-year-old trader from Richmond

'Phew – what a few months I've had. I've just looked in my diary and seen I have rarely had an empty evening, yet it's been blissful. I cannot apologise enough for how difficult I've been to get hold of since I registered with you – I promise I'm never normally as busy as I have been, but you only have your advice to thank for that!'

Sarah, 42-year-old business consultant from Central London

'Can I just say that although I was a little miffed at your comments on my evaluation report, and told you so in no uncertain terms after I came to see you six months ago, you were absolutely spot on. I have been following your advice and things have changed for the better for me. I have not met my soul mate yet, but I have to say it feels like it will only be a matter of time. So a big thank you from someone I bet you least expected to hear from again.'

Petra, 45-year-old part-time charity worker from Oxford

'Hope everything's good with you. Things with Stefan, the man you introduced me to five months ago, are fantastic. He's such a sweet guy. Last night I met his brother and wife – they were just lovely to me. So can I now place things on hold with other guys? I know you say keep your options open, and I have, but Stefan is looking like proper boyfriend material now and introduces me to everyone as his 'partner'! Thank you so much for finding him; he really is so great! He's very keen which, ordinarily, would put me off but because I like him, it doesn't. But I have to say I have completely relaxed and taken your advice and been a bit of a challenge, as you put it (and it does seem to make him more keen!).

It feels so easy – wish I had met you years ago as it probably would have saved a lot of heartache.

Oh – and so many of my friends have seen how happy I am with Stefan and have all asked for your details, so you'll probably get an influx of people mailing you!

Once again – thank you so much for all your help, advice and for finding Stefan. Who knows, maybe I will end up settling down and having a family after all; I had just about given up hope.'

Charlotte, 35-year-old lawyer from Highgate

'Lorraine after all the help and advice you have given to me over the past two years, and continued helping me through the early months of my relationship with Sean, we wondered if you could introduce any nice young ladies to his son who is 28 and heartbroken after his girlfriend left him for another man.'

Verity, 51-year-old accountant from Essex

'Lorraine you will be so proud of me, I have organised myself three dates this month through online dating, in addition to the one you have organised for me. I feel twenty years younger and have taken all your advice on board. I am not in the least bit nervous even though these will be the first dates I have been on in seven years. I am so grateful to you; I feel like a new woman.'

Roz, 52-year-old nurse from Reading

'Just wanted to drop you a note to say your seminar has really changed my attitude to dating and life in general and I am feeling so much the happier for it ... (And dating someone, but keeping a level head.)' I am halfway through the book you recommended, Why Men Love Bitches, and it's excellent! Thanks again.'

Annette, 37-year-old lawyer from London

'Thank you for your guide on Internet dating. I followed it to the letter and after nearly a year of dismal dating I am now getting regular requests to meet.'

Supriya, 34-year-old jewellery designer from Birmingham

'I just read your evaluation report for me. I feel after just over an hour's session you seem to have understood me better than my own mother. On reflection I can see where I have been going wrong, and I can tell you I will bow down to your guidance from now on. I await my first instructions.'

Penny, 36-year-old IT worker from Reading

'Lorraine your advice has been invaluable; Peter and I would like to invite you to our wedding next June!'

Denise, 49-year-old entrepreneur from Docklands

'You have given me so much confidence. I have started to make an effort in the mornings when I go to work and quietened down in the pub with the lads after work, and just like you said, the guys have actually started flirting with me. The one I liked emailed me today to ask if I was wanted to go to a client party with him. I remembered what you said about posing myself as a challenge and sent an email back to say yes as long as he didn't expect me to treat it as a date. He emailed straight back and said no because he would like to take me for a real date the following Saturday! So the guy I have been making eyes at for nearly 18 months finally made a move when I stepped back, just as you predicted. You are a marvel.'

Lucy, 29-year-old PR consultant from Putney

'Lorraine, emailing you from Canada where we are both living now since marrying just after Christmas. We thought you should be one of the first to know we are also expecting our first baby in February next year. I know I have thanked you a million times, but here is a big thank you again for the million and one time.'

Julia 39 and Blake 44

'James and I are officially an item. Lorraine, thank you for pushing me to meet him even though I was adamant when you suggested him to me that he wasn't my type! Please don't ever tell him that...he, James, is different from anyone I have ever met, and that's probably why he is the longest relationship I've ever had (bar the two year relationship I had when I was 15!). We are buying a place together this year and I am hopeful I have finally met my match.'

Beverly 33 model and part time TV presenter London

Appendix Two

Lorraine's Little Black Book
– the dating sites and
services that you can't
live without

Appendix Two Lorraine's Little Black Book – the dating sites and services that you can't live without

It's always helpful to have recommendations when you are looking to try something new and that's exactly what you will find here. With my knowledge of the industry I know the sites and services that are worth trying and those where you will be wasting your time. When it comes to online dating, most of the big sites you see advertised on TV are going to be huge, generic sites, with an anything goes approach. They may be inexpensive, but they are rarely going to produce anyone super dynamic.

You have to ask yourself – if I were to go out and socialise, would I choose somewhere where most likely there will be just your average people? Or would I rather go somewhere a little more up market and niche? Whatever your preference, apply the same philosophy to online dating. Yes, there are millions of people to choose from on the huge sites, but it is a little like looking for a needle in a haystack, whereas with the smaller, more niche sites you have a better chance of finding more likeminded people.

Some of the smaller sites are also for more specific audiences, such as sites for single parents, or if you prefer to meet men with a sense of responsibility, sites for the military and ex-soldiers. Just because these sites are niche it doesn't usually mean they are more expensive. You simply don't hear about them because the larger sights have massive marketing and advertising budgets. Below is a guide to the companies that, in my opinion, offer the best services.

- The best large online site is without a doubt **www.smooch.com**.
  Unlike the other mass marketed sites it's completely free. You can search and contact other users and you can chat and exchange as many messages as you like. They also have additional features. For example, they have the amazing 'Intro Analytics' system, which is a unique recommendation engine for people matching. It works by using algorithms, which are based on a combination of machine learning and psychology, to accurately identify people's tastes. When you make a search, it considers your choices and builds up a picture of your likes and dislikes. The more you search, the more additional people it will flag up to you. This feature saves so much time, especially as the database is huge. www.smooch.com is a national dating site, and well worth trying.

- If you are into fitness, a good niche site is **www.fitness-singles.com**. It originated in the USA and is doing well over here with a good calibre of members. Usually you will find that men who are of fit body are also of fit mind. Guys who are dedicated enough to regularly follow and partake in sport are most often driven successful individuals.

- **www.gorgeousnetworks.com** is a fabulous site; I know because I launched it in 2000! It has always attracted appealing, driven individuals. The age range is around 28–45. The online dating club has a door policy, which is managed by its members, so only people who the members deem are 'gorgeous' are invited to join. The site has never attracted model-type airheads: gorgeous is defined by what they have going for them, so members tend to have a combination of looks, presence and drive. The clientele is predominantly professional, business types located mostly in London and the big cities who are usually well travelled and sporty. The site can also be accessed through **www.thegorgeousnetwork.com**.

- If you are slightly older **www.guardiansoulmates.com** is a good choice. It is not necessarily full of left-wing Guardian readers; you will find arty, cultured professionals mainly in their 40s through to 60s.

- **www.topdreamdates.com** is a fabulous site for dipping your toe into the dating scene. You just list the type of date you would fancy going on, wait to see who responds, and then take up the most appealing offer. It is also a good site if you have tickets for somewhere – a sporting event or theatre – perfect to get a one off date. If things materialise great, but with this site there is no pressure.

- **www.citysocialising.com** – a similar concept to www.topdreamdates.com.

- Another popular site is **www.makefriendsonline.com**, which is a national site with good calibre people who are mainly in their 30s through to 50s.

- If you are looking for masculine types then try **www.forcespenpals.co.uk**.

- The best and biggest site in Ireland is **www.anotherfriend.com**.

- For quick flirts and mobile phone dating try **www.flirtomatic.com** – a great site for brushing up on your flirting skills.

- **www.datingforparents.com** is a good starting point if you have small children, as you will find sympathetic men who are perhaps in a similar position.

- A fantastic site used predominantly by the Asian community is **www.asiansinglesolution.com**.

Personal Introductions

www.coffeeandcompany.com organises coffee dates for members. The client base is predominantly executive types in their 30s through to 50-plus. The service is very professional and the team headhunt additional people for their clients to meet rather than rely on the pool of people in the database. Guidance and feedback is all part of the service. You can also book a one to one Personal Dating Evaluation with a romance expert at Coffee and Company.

Suggested reading and audio material

- *Why Men Love Bitches* by Sherry Argov – great for keeping you posed as a challenge to all mankind.

- *Mama Gena's School of Womanly Arts* by Regena Thomashauer – this book does what it says on the cover and will help you develop your female charms.

- *Keeping the Love you Find* by Harville Hendrix – is a must if you are a little lost. Finding yourself is very important before trying to find a partner.

- For positive thinking the best books available are *Cosmic Ordering in 7 Easy Steps* by Carolyn Boyes followed by *The Secret* by Rhonda Byrne (though you may find the DVD of *The Secret* more easy to follow).

- I also suggest Edgar Cayce's great motivating CD *Self Hypnosis*.

Gyms

I wholeheartedly recommend you join a gym. It's a great place to meet men, it will keep you fit and in good shape and it's an added interest to bag. The chain gyms are great but the exclusive gyms are even better. You get what you pay for. One of the best is the Chelsea club at Stamford Bridge. It is expensive but worth it and works out good value for money. Look at the local gyms and make sure the people attending are your type of people.

To keep up to date with my recommendations on where to go, what to do, what to read and more, go to **www.calcudating.com**